THE CONVERSION

OF

THE NORTHERN NATIONS.

THE CONVERSION

OF

THE NORTHERN NATIONS.

THE

BOYLE LECTURES

FOR THE YEAR 1865,

DELIVERED AT THE CHAPEL ROYAL, WHITEHALL.

BY

CHARLES MERIVALE, B.D.,

RECTOR OF LAWFORD; CHAPLAIN TO THE SPEAKER OF THE HOUSE OF COMMONS.
AUTHOR OF "A HISTORY OF THE ROMANS UNDER THE EMPIRE."

NEW YORK:
D. APPLETON AND COMPANY,
443 & 445 BROADWAY.
1866.

PREFACE.

THE discourses which were delivered at the Boyle Lecture in the present year were intended to be a continuation of those of the year preceding, on the Conversion of the Roman Empire. It had been justly remarked that in my earlier course I had treated principally of the preparation of the heathen world for the reception of Christianity, and had said too little of the progress of thought and opinion among the Christians themselves, which led to that development of Nicene theology to which I had pointed as the goal of Pagan conversion. Without pledging myself at the time to carry on my historical view to the conversion of the Northern Nations, such had been from the first my wish and distant object; and I already contemplated giving such a sketch of the progress of dogma within the Church as might correspond with that of the revolution of religious opinion without it. I make this remark now, superfluous though it may perhaps be, in order to explain why a series of discourses, to which I have given the general title of the 'Conversion of the Northern Nations,' commences with three at least, the subject of which may seem more closely connected with the earlier course than with the present. But in fact I wish the two little volumes to be regarded as one work; and if at some future time I may have the opportunity of printing them together, I shall probably give them the general title of the 'Conversion of the Ancient Heathens.'

The main object of both these courses of lectures has been to impress upon the hearer or reader the conviction, which must be ever present to the mind of one who is accustomed to study the broad features of human history, of the gradual and constant preparation of mankind, from the earliest known periods of antiquity, for the full development of religious life under the revelation of Jesus Christ. It is well to hold fast the assurance of the continuity of God's providence in the spiritual guidance of our species; to be convinced that, as we can discover no entirely new creation in the progress of material things since the first beginning we can trace of them, so neither has there been any entirely new moral or religious revelation vouchsafed to us. The same God has been over all His works, both the material and the spiritual, from the beginning, animating, amending, informing, indoctrinating His moral creation, from time to time, in an appointed order and sequence, but never entirely breaking with the past, and effecting a new creation without using the materials of the old. Our religion is an historical one: it is the history of religious progress. The Scriptures of the Old and the New Testament testify to a progressive development of Divine Truth. The verities imparted to the patriarchs are still the foundation of the religion of Jesus Christ; and the religious notions of the Heathens, which seem to be themselves corruptions of the verities imparted to the patriarchs, or dim reflections of that Light which lighteth every man that cometh into the world, may well deserve to be regarded with interest, to be criticized with love and even with reverence. As in my former lectures I thought it right and just to show, as far as I might, the elements of truth and goodness disseminated among the benighted votaries of the imperial schools and temples, so in these I have not shrunk from indicating the thread of moral and religious feeling which runs through the grovelling superstitions and intellectual darkness even of the Northern barbarians.

My limits, indeed, have been extremely narrow, and I cannot but acknowledge that I leave the subject, even in the rude sketch to which the conditions of the place and the occasion confined me, to the full as imperfect, and as abruptly concluded, as that to which I applied myself in the preceding year. If I seem to any to have trifled with a matter of real importance, I can only throw myself again on the indulgence which was before extended to me, while I hope at least that even such slight sketches as these may suffice to awaken an interest in the subject, in the minds of some who have ability and learning to prosecute it more worthily.

CONTENTS.

LECTURE I.

THE PHILOSOPHICAL VIEW OF CHRIST'S REVELATION: JUSTIN MARTYR AND CLEMENT OF ALEXANDRIA.

1 CORINTH IX. 3.

Mine answer to them that do examine me is this.

THE discourses I delivered in this place last year were meant to recommend the truth of the Christian Religion from regard to the influence it exerted on the mind and conscience of the Pagans under the Roman Empire. To them, as I then showed, it approved itself a message of love and peace; it explained their sense of weariness and disgust with life; it probed their hearts, and disclosed to them the full iniquity of sinfulness; it aroused, and again it allayed, their spiritual terrors; it set God before them in his moral and spiritual nature; it showed them the beauty of holiness upon earth, and led their hopes and aspirations onwards to the consummation of holiness hereafter in a future life conformed to His image who is Himself the Holy One and the Just.

That the inference I suggested from these considerations is by no means conclusively established by them I could not be unaware. To show that the Gospel harmonizes with the feelings of human nature could be no direct proof of its direct and special revelation from God. The argument, it has been said, is two-edged. If it be urged, on the one hand, that God sent His message to men purposely in such a form as would naturally attract and convince the beings whom He meant to save by it,—on the other hand it may be contended that the correspondence of the Gospel with man's wants and wishes shows how possibly, how probably, man may have invented it for himself.

This objection is an obvious, and no doubt a plausible one. That there is some force in it we must admit; for otherwise the argument on the Christian side would amount to a demonstration, a conclusion to which God in His inscrutable wisdom has not allowed any of the moral arguments in favor of revelation to arrive.

But if we admit—which is more than can be required of us—that the conscience of some among the unconverted heathens was as deeply moved as that of the true believers:—that Seneca, for instance, felt the same deep-grounded conflict between the Flesh and the Spirit as St. Paul; that Aurelius yearned with the same tender love towards God and man as the disciple whom Jesus Himself loved; that Epictetus or Dion was as bold and ardent in the assurance of his faith as Peter:—if we allow that all the fulness, all the strength of the Christian character are shown forth (which is surely going far beyond the mark) in one virtuous Heathen or another: —does it follow that because Seneca was thus haply moved by nature, Paul therefore was not moved by grace; because the Platonists and the Stoics were mere human teachers, the Church of Christ has no higher sanction for its teaching, no holier Spirit to animate it, than they had? Not so: Seneca lived, and preached, and died in his faith, and left no seed after him. Aurelius lived, and preached, and died in his faith, and left no seed after him. The Stoics and the Platonists lived and preached, and they died in their faith; but they too left no seed after them. There was evidently something wanting to them, some principle of force to convince and constrain men, some power creative of new feelings and impulses, some harmony with God, some sympathy with the grace proceeding from His Spirit.

We may trace, then, among the holy men of Paganism a certain receptivity of Gospel truth; but we cannot trace, I think, any power to imagine and invent it. If so, the argument for Christianity from its manifest adaptation to the wants of the age to which it was first addressed has its proper force. It is to be used temperately, to be guarded cautiously; but it is not to be surrendered at a captious demand; it is not to be discarded weakly and distrustfully. It has done good service at all periods of the great Christian controversy, and it will still continue to serve us. It gains force by accumulation, it strengthens itself with time.

The men of thought and feeling among the Heathens of the Empire, whose conversion was one of the first great triumphs of Christian truth, were not the only generation or class of men who have recognized the harmony between human longings and divine teachings. God has spoken to man through His Church at sundry times and in divers manners, appealing here to the educated and intellectual, there to the rude and uncultivated, here to the hopes, there to the fears of men, here to the sober thoughtfulness of a fixed and mature civilization, there to the buoyant ardour of a wandering forest-tribe; and in all these and other phases of human society, He has found witnesses to the agreement of His Truth, and of His Truth only, with the common needs and yearnings of His creatures. We cannot say that he has raised Himself such witnesses everywhere. There is perhaps no harder trial of our faith than the fact of the apparent failure of God's Word, here and there at least, among the most refined of the civilized, as among the wildest of the savage,—among the Chinese, for instance, as among the Hottentots,—to strike the chord of sympathy by which, as we must believe, all the nations of the earth are actually bound together. But few studies can be more interesting, few arguments for our religion have generally been found more attractive, than those which seek to trace the influence of Christianity upon minds just awakened to its teaching; the preparation for its reception which it finds already in them, and the vivifying energy with which it inspires and fructifies them.

The triumph, indeed, of Christianity over the prejudices of the philosophers was, I think, more rapid, more striking, than has generally been supposed. We have allowed too much force to the statement of St. Jerome, rhetorical and artful as his statements too often are, of the smallness of the number of the wise and learned among the leaders and teachers of the Church of Christ. Traces are not wanting of the reception of the Gospel by a multitude of the educated classes even in the first and second centuries. But we must remember that, whatever their number, such converts did not generally make themselves prominent, either in doing or in suffering. It is not among them, generally, that we find the leaders and martyrs of the early Church. It is not among such that we find the leaders and the martyrs of any Church. In periods of spiritual revolution, when new religious ideas are painfully but hopefully struggling against old traditions, fortified by power and prejudice, the men who dare most are not generally those who think and reflect most. Action springs from feeling rather than from reflection. Beholding with awe and wonder the grandeur and solidity of the Pagan religion and of the Pagan polity, of the Pontiff and of the Emperor, under a Nero or a Trajan, such men might say to themselves, 'This work we have taken in hand is God's work, not man's work; man can do little or nothing in it: God can do all, and doubtless will do all! How can the Christian meet the philosopher? What common ground of argument can they discover? How shall faith encounter reason? What fellowship hath light with darkness? How shall we meet the man of the world, the politician, the voluptuary? What arguments can arrest the light and thoughtless votaries of a world of sense: the enthusiasts of these brilliant idolatries, who have found in the hymns, the pomps, the shows of all-embracing Heathenism all that their heart, all that their conscience requires?'

'Let us leave,' so they would say, 'the issue to God, let us turn ourselves quietly and privately to Him, and bury ourselves in Christ from the world, that we may rise again with Christ. Let Him show Himself if He will. Let Him assert Himself, and avenge Himself in His own way, in His own time. Let God look to His own honour; as the Heathen himself has said, "God's honour is his own great concern."'

There is reason to believe that even in the pure and ardent era of early Christianity there was much of this spirit of quietism and apathy among the converts from the patrician classes of Rome. It was not of such stuff, indeed, that the martyrs and confessors, and bold declaimers of the persecuted Church were made. These were generally less polished, less fastidious, less selfish, if you will. They did the real work of their Master; and they have left the impress of their character on the work; so much so that we are apt to suppose that they constituted the whole of the Christian society, and to overlook the fund of intelligent but more passive belief which lay behind them. For see how, as soon as the first fierceness of hatred and persecution relaxed, our records begin to teem with names of the learned and the intellectual. The Christian enjoyed a respite under Hadrian. The Emperor was himself learned and a patron of learning; he was anxious about the learning of all sects, and he pried even into the doctrines of the Christian Church. Immediately the schools of Athens were filled with converted philosophers. Justin, himself eventually a martyr, leads the van; and is followed by a Tatian, an Athenagoras, a Quadratus, a Theophilus. These were the first apologists, and some of them gave at last their lives for the faith they had defended; but it was an interval of sunshine, a moment of ease and presumed security, that brought them to light; that brought to light, in short, the capacity of the Christian doctrine to attract, to interest, to sway unto itself the foremost thinkers of the age. Then follows another period of persecution, and the learning of the Christians seems again to shrink behind a cloud. Free thought is again restored half a century later, and is marked at once by an outburst of intellectual vigour among the great assertors of the Faith, which may favourably compare even with the flower of Heathen intelligence. In Clement of Alexandria, in Tertullian, in Origen, it is clear that the battle has been won. The loftiest minds have ranged themselves on the side of the Gospel; the Spirit leads them, and victory follows them. The most comprehensive acquirements, the subtlest acumen, the most liberal and enlightened sympathies, have become enlisted in the cause of the divine Jesus.

Now it is to be observed that it was not till the battle had been nearly won—not till the Gospel had attained a manifest vantage ground, and Paganism was beginning to totter under its long and pertinacious assaults—that the apologists of the early Church resorted generally to a direct attack on its flagrant absurdities and corruptions. It was a sign that they felt themselves secure of God's triumph when they fiercely ascribed all Paganism to the immediate promptings of the devil. But this was not the line of argument adopted while the issue might seem yet in the balance; nor was it commonly at any time the line adopted by the converts from the ranks of the Pagan philosophers. Generally, it was the line of men who had been born Christians, not of men who had become Christians; of men who had been bred from infancy in hatred and contempt of the forms of thought which were passing away, not of those who with many an effort and in much agony of spirit had cast off the cherished love of youth and manhood, and surrendered their dearest prejudices for the promise of divine enlightenment. The man who felt his Pagan speculations transfigured into Christian faith, essayed to exalt, to spiritualize, to harmonize with Gospel truth the aspirations of his early masters. He showed forth the divine character of Christ's teaching, as the ideal to which human imaginations had been ever tending; he represented Christ as the incarnation of an idea for which man, through the unconscious working of divine grace in his heart, had been ever yearning and grasping. He rejoiced in tracing among the utterances of the good and wise throughout the world, throughout time, the faint anticipations of redemption and glory by which God had never left Himself wholly without a witness among the creatures He loves and cherishes.

It was, I say, in the intervals of early persecution, while the sword was yet suspended, while the issue was yet doubtful, while it was the first interest of the believers to make a favourable impression, that the Christian thinkers—such names as I have mentioned—rushed forward to conciliate opinions, to harmonize truths and convictions. They did not shrink in fear or hatred from the Pagans; they did not bury themselves sullenly in their own reflections, nor fall back unsociably on their personal hopes and assurances; least of all did they now taunt and defy the strong but slumbering adversary. No: they came forward, with eager heart and hand extended, to invite and welcome the Pagans; to make them one with themselves in love, one in hope, one even in favour with a common Father and Sanctifier and Redeemer. They were resolved, it would seem, to bring into discredit the vulgar charge against them, of fleeing the light, of hating their fellowmen, of living for themselves in their inner circle only, and surrendering the outer world complacently to divine wrath and inevitable condemnation.

To mark from our own distant standing-point the agreement of Christian truth with the wants and imaginations of religious men among the Pagans, was the object of my former lectures in this place; and the same observation was made in ancient times by one school at least of the early apologists. The influence to which I pointed was felt to be forcible then, as we believe it to be forcible now. But the argument has a special interest in the mouths of men like Justin and his colleagues, who had issued themselves from the schools of Pagan philosophy, and had tasted it in its strength and its weakness, its truth and its errors.

Justin the Martyr, of whom I would first speak as the representative of this school of Christian Apology, came forth from the old university of Heathen Athens, the nurse and mistress of antique tradition, tenacious of the accustomed forms of thought, still brooding over the memories of the past, retrospective in its views, conservative in its feelings, still jealously grasping the thread of continuity which seemed to the last to connect the speculations of the present with the speculations of seven restless centuries before it. Justin had himself disputed in the school of Plato; he spoke the language of Plato, he wore the dress of Plato, he was imbued with the spirit while he cherished the outward tokens of the old Pagan thought on which so many ardent souls had seemed to soar onwards and upwards. All these dreams have been his—his the hope, the rapture; his again the disappointment, the disenchantment: but his hope has been rekindled, his rapture revived; and conviction not to be abandoned, faith never to be ashamed of, have in his case, as of one among myriads, succeeded to the despair which clouded the vision of his predecessors. Persuaded of the new, he cannot yet relinquish the old. Though a disciple of John, he remembers Plato; though a worshipper of Christ, he reverences Socrates; though a student of the Gospel, he feels the teachings of Nature, and hears the voice of the human conscience, and traces from generation to generation the trail of divine illumination. He regards Christianity as the last crowning development of holy Philosophy, the severest and most perfect image of God's transcendent nature, the abiding witness to His eternal Truth.

The idea which was present to the mind of the Athenian sages, which was rendered concrete under the appellation of the Word, has become a personal incarnation in the rapt vision of the Apostle John, and is accepted as the divine Son of God by Justin, his disciple. The Word, Justin believes, has been made Flesh, and dwelt as a divine person among us. Not only does he believe: he admires, he loves the Word, he falls down before Him and worships Him. He worships 'the Word of God, eternal and ineffable, who was made man that He might heal us by partaking of our sufferings.' His belief is direct and positive. He holds it distinct from the arbitrary fancies of the Gnostics, whose theory of Æons and Emanations was a mere nominal recognition of shadowy and factitious Existences. He maintains that Jesus Christ is the only Son of God, who dwells in the bosom of the Father.

This Word, which is thus no mere Idea, but a living Being, is not the less the Wisdom and Reason of God, the Reason living and acting. It lighteth every man that cometh into the world: all creatures endowed with intelligence and will partake of its sovereign nature. 'The seed of the Word,' he declares, 'is sown in every reasonable creature.' But the Word is not Intelligence only. It is the source of all Good as well as of all Knowledge. It is the principle of Life, moral as well as intellectual: it is the substance of the superior Life which exists in all free and responsible beings. And thus does Justin, Christian as he is, attach himself to all the great and good men of antiquity. He remarks the influence of the Word on the wisest and bravest spirits of Greece and Rome, as well as of Israel and Judah. He detects God's reflection in the teaching of the Porch, as well as in the Shechinah of the Temple. All, in his view, who have lived conformably to the Word are Christians in nature though not in name. Such have been Socrates and Heraclitus among the Pagans—Socrates has himself *known Christ:* such have been Abraham and Elias and Ananias among the Jews; such have been Paul and John; such are now the saints and confessors of the Gospel in this latter generation. Those who have opposed the Reason and the Word—alas! the bulk of mankind—were Anti-christs, long before the advent and ministry of Christ himself; the murderers of the men of good-will towards Him, even the best and wisest of the Heathens, who lived according to His truth. Martyrs there have been before Stephen: Saints there have been before the Baptist. To the Pagans Justin could apply the language with which Christ had scathed the iniquity of the Pharisees: 'Ye who build the sepulchres of the Prophets, ye have slain them yourselves.' For the Pagans too, in their day, had slain or persecuted the teachers whom they afterwards exalted and canonized.

But our Christian philosopher is not content to dwell on these general analogies. His creed is no mere rhetorical flourish. He sets himself earnestly to teach us wherein these preludes to Christianity consisted, and to disentangle them from the errors and superstitions which had overlaid them. Belief in Immortality, belief in a Resurrection, expectation of a Judgment to come, of punishment and rewards—such, he says, with all the fables and follies that have disgraced or encumbered them, are the Christian truths to which the eyes of the best and wisest of the Heathens had been already opened by the Spirit of Grace. Even the vulgar religion of the multitude bears a precious testimony in his eyes to the eternal verities first revealed by God to the patriarchs. God has thus never left Himself without witness in the hearts of His creatures. He has never abandoned the fallen world which He once for all created for His Glory.

There is assuredly a breadth and liberality of feeling in this view of the common inheritance of Gospel Truth which must ever be attractive and interesting. It seems to smooth some of the harshest difficulties of religion; to soothe some of the sharpest pangs of humanity. But it will not, after all, admit of being pushed to extremity; and its intrinsic weakness becomes apparent even in the feebleness and indecision of the teacher himself, when he proceeds to follow it into particular details. He has been led to the brink of an argument in defence of the grossest monstrosities of Heathen mythology. He starts back dismayed at his own indiscretion. The great apostle might point with daring finger to the altar of the Unknown God at Athens, and claim it as an anticipation of a divine revelation; but it becomes none of his humble followers to make so bold an application. God alone knows who are His, and what human ideas are the reflection of divine Truths. He can inspire His appointed preachers to discover and bring them to light; but Justin, at least, is too modest to assume the mantle of the inspired. He leaves it to a later school and a more confident generation to proclaim the universality of the Gospel.

Such a school, and such a generation, were indeed to make their appearance; to prosecute these same views with a difference; in some respects to give them a legitimate development, in others to expand them into extravagance and folly. We pass on to the next great name among the early defenders of Christianity, the most learned, the most ingenious perhaps of all, to Clement of Alexandria.

The city wherein this illustrious doctor first learned and afterwards abjured the philosophies of Paganism, stood in marked contrast with Athens as a place of spiritual training. Alexandria also was a vast Pagan university; but it was a school of progress and inquiry rather than of retrospection and tradition. It embraced with ardour new opinions; it welcomed foreign speculations. It opened its arms to the teachers of Judaism, and again to the teachers of Gnosticism. It could admire the fanatic monotheism of Arabia, and look beyond it to the labyrinthine intricacies of Hindoo theology. In the vast libraries which it collected, and to which it invited the students of every nation, it combined and assimilated all science, all theory, and fused together the belief of every age and country, to form, perchance, the basis of some new creed, yet undeveloped, for all ages and for all countries. The doctors of Alexandria, when converted to Christianity, were not constrained by early love and sympathy to look fondly back to the teaching of the Grecian schools as the foundation, not to be relinquished, of all spiritual Truth—to seek, above all things, to harmonize them with the new and higher teaching to which they had been admitted. Still less had they any lingering loyalty to the vanities of Pagan mythology, or the pretensions of the Pagan mysteries to explain and justify them. The age of Clement, one generation later than that of Justin, was marked indeed, in this respect, by special characteristics. Christianity had advanced a stage in its progress. It had assumed the offensive against Paganism, and had forced the Pagans to scan earnestly and impatiently the grounds of their old beliefs. Their religion had been rudely shaken; its absurdities had been laid bare. Its upholders had been compelled to reconsider their position, and to seek on all hands the means of maintaining it. Paganism, awakened to the consciousness of its internal weakness, was affecting boldness to smother its rising doubts and apprehensions. The temples were renovated, the idols were freshly decked, the sacrifices were redoubled; shrines, oracles, and prodigies were fanatically sought after. The flame was flickering in its socket, and burning with fitful vehemence in these latter moments of its existence. It is to this reaction of Paganism that Clement directly addresses himself. A great part of his Apologies is framed for the bold exposure of the hollowness of the old beliefs, and shows how strong the Christians now were in their position; that they could become assailants in their turn; that in the great cosmopolitan capital at least they could speak and be listened to, and that Truth, unfettered, was marching on straight to triumph.

But it was perhaps this very feeling of security, this assurance of ultimate success, that led a thoughtful Christian like the father before us to look with consideration and indulgence on the errors of human nature. Clement hates and mocks at Paganism; but he loves and pities the Pagans. He seeks for no communion, he admits of no communion, between the Gospel and the old mythology; but he recognizes the votaries of Olympus as fellows with the worshippers of Olivet. He bows with no excessive reverence before the teachers of the Porch or the Academy; yet he hails them as brothers in love and intelligence with the disciples who issued to convert the world from an upper chamber of the Temple. Sprung himself from no special school of thought and inquiry, he is sworn to the teaching of no individual master; but he regards every effort of the human soul in search of truth as informed with grace from above, as prompted by that Divine Author to whom it ultimately leads. He is genial and universal in his sympathies with his fellowmen. Every art, he says, springs from God; every exercise of intelligence raises men towards God. That true idea of divinity which has been at length revealed by direct communication from above, the imagination of poets and artists no less than of philosophers, has ever been striving to realize. Christ has been the Desired of all nations, even when they knew not their own desire. To all men purified and prepared by this desire, the Word now reveals Himself by grace, and this revelation is finally confirmed by the witness of the Holy Spirit in the Scriptures. The proof of God's truth, he says, must be a moral one: the witness of miracles and of prophecy is external and subsidiary only.

If Justin sought, then, to make terms with the philosophers as his own fellow-labourers and colleagues, by showing them that they had been themselves preaching the Word unwittingly, Clement, as one of the multitude, as himself an outsider, consoles and cheers the multitude, by proving that, with all their errors and shortcomings,

God has never quite forsaken them, but has been ever leading them all onwards as an indulgent father, has been ever training them, by every thought and word and action and aspiration of their uninformed intelligence, to love Him with the love which casteth out shame and fear and self-reproach. They too have all been doing the work which was given them to do, they too have been faithful over a little: and now He comes with a joyful message to His faithful ones, 'Enter ye into the joy of your Lord.'

Such, I believe, is a fair representation of the general tone of our earliest apologetics. Their common object was to connect the Christian Revelation with the general development of man's moral and spiritual nature. The school of Justin traced this development mainly in the formal teaching of the sects; the school of Clement recognized it further in the universal tendencies of human nature. Both defended and explained the Gospel on the ground of its agreement with God's eternal teachings, as though in its descent from heaven no new or strange thing had happened unto us, but such only as was the proper end and issue of the spiritual education of His creatures. It is evident that the defence was commonly admitted, the explanation widely appreciated. The answer of the early apologists unto them that examined them was this—the same which has been repeated from age to age, the same which I have before advanced in this place, and which I began this discourse by asserting—that the truth of God's Holy Word may be known from its agreement with the conscience, its answer to the questionings of man. A sober and earnest belief in the depth and breadth of the foundations of our Lord's revelation must lead us at all times to see in it the completion and crown of human speculation; not the sworn antagonist of philosophy and science, but their ally and friend, their leader and their guide.

But we must not stop here; and the defect of these early apologists must have been already apparent to you, that they were too much inclined to stop here. In showing how much Christianity agreed with human thought, they were in danger of overlooking the points in which it lay beside it and above it. Regarding it as the companion, or at least the complement of philosophy, they forgot or disregarded the fact that it is a further revelation of things beyond philosophy. Not that Justin, still less that Clement, fail to signalize the divine character of its Founder, or neglect the fundamental incidents of His history, or suppress the miraculous tokens by which His ministry was accompanied. No Christian teacher of the early Church dared to represent Jesus, as some moderns represent him, as a mere man, a wiser Socrates, a holier Plato, a more consistent Seneca. It was from the defect of their position, as individual inquirers, not yet trained to accept the concurrent tradition of the Church, of the many teaching as one, that they scanned the Christian dogma thus partially and obliquely. The time was not yet ripe for its full and consistent exposition. The great doctrines of the Divine Nature, of Salvation, and of

Grace, are of no private interpretation. The discrimination of the Persons of the Godhead was as yet unsteady and fluctuating. Christ was commonly regarded as man's champion against the Devil, as his raiser from the Fall, rather than his Redeemer from Sin, and his Reconciler with his Judge; grace was extenuated too much as a universal inheritance, instead of being proclaimed as the special gift of the Spirit unto them that believe. Large and generous was the teaching of the schools before us; it may easily dazzle us with its brilliancy, it may kindle in us a glow of sympathy and admiration. But we must examine it with caution; we must accept it with some qualification. It has in it much truth, even of the highest truth; but it is not all true, nor is it all the truth. Its obliquities and defects became from day to day apparent. As it sprang directly from the interpretation of the Grecian schools, so it leaned too favourably to mere Grecian modes of speculation; it allied itself too closely with the ideas of classical philosophy. But God had other races of men, other habits of mind and spiritual training, to bring into the confession of faith in Him and in His Gospel; and He required the teaching of his word to be placed upon a broader foundation, to be developed from a deeper source; that Christ might become the Desire of another people, the Light and Life of a new world of humanity.

LECTURE II.

THE PRACTICAL VIEW OF CHRIST'S REVELATION: TERTULLIAN AND ORIGEN.

1 CORINTH. IX. 3.

Mine answer to them that do examine me is this.

IN my first lecture I showed how the truths of Christian Revelation proved themselves attractive to the highest order of intelligence among the Heathens; how some of the most devout and eloquent defenders of the Gospel arose in the Pagan schools of Athens and Alexandria, and mounted from the chairs of philosophers to the pulpit of Christian preachers. It was natural that such converts, men of mature minds and long-formed habits of thought, while submitting the wisdom they had learned from their masters to the higher wisdom of Christ, should feel unwilling—should indeed be morally unable—to renounce all the spiritual truths on which their souls had so long been nourished.

Does any one of us in mid-life find himself constrained to change his earlier views on moral, or religious, or political questions? His first care is, I suppose, always to justify his change to himself by seeking to deduce it legitimately from his original principles. He rejects one development as a wrong one; he accepts another as the right; but the principle he still maintains was right from the first. And so the converted philosophers were intent, as we have seen, on showing that the new victorious faith was itself based upon the same eternal verities as those on which their own confused reasonings had been founded; and sprang from the same Divine Author, the guide whose footsteps they had ever traced, however inconsistently and feebly. Each reverted to his first foundations, having cleared away the Pagan superstructure, and erected upon them the Christian edifice which seemed to his own conscience to accord with them.

Among Christian thinkers and teachers, Justin and Clement, the Athenian and the Alexandrian, will always have their followers and successors. The worth of the human understanding, the claims of human speculation, will always attach to themselves patrons. We shall always hear among us the praises of human excellence, familiar to us in the language of the greatest master of secular eloquence: 'What a piece of work is man! How noble in reason, how infinite in faculties! In form and moving how express and admirable! in action how like an angel! in apprehension how like a God!' We shall press to our hearts with pride and self-complacency the liberal admission of an inspired preacher, that 'that which may be known of God is manifest' even in the Heathen: 'for the invisible things of Him from the creation of the world are clearly seen, being understood by the things that are made:' and that men, even in the valley of the shadow of heathenism and idolatry, still 'knew God,' even when they 'glorified Him not as God.' Accordingly there will be a constant effort to show that the discoveries of the human mind in the domain of the moral and the spiritual have been sound and substantial; and that the highest proof of the divinity of Christ's final Revelation is the sanction it gives, the confirmation it extends, to the anticipations of the human understanding. One school of Apologists will insist upon the essential harmony between the Gospel of the Lord Jesus and the teachings of a Plato; another will argue that from age to age the imagination of man was brooding on religious anticipations, faintly sketching its dim glimpses of the future, prophesying of the glory that was to be revealed at the end.

This argument, shadowy and imperfect though it be, is doubtless fraught with the spirit of truth, and the souls which pleaded with it have not sought its succour in vain. This is one of the many answers we may give to them that examine us touching the grounds of our faith in Christ. He has hallowed human philosophy. He has responded to human aspirations and auguries. Man has been prepared through long ages for His advent, and for the Revelation of the Faith in Him. Justin and Clement may still stand in the breach for us: not clothed in the whole armour of God, but at least with utterance given unto them to open their mouth boldly, to make known the mystery of the Gospel.

But we admit the obvious dangers of this attractive argument: we know how apt men are to build too much upon it, to yield too indolently to it, to look too exclusively towards it. We know that the Heathen may use it for his own purposes, to fortify his own pride and confirm him in his self-sufficiency; and he may stop short abruptly in the career along which we would lead him, and refuse to acknowledge the conclusions to which we would compel him. We know further, that it may tempt the Christian also, the imperfect or nominal believer, to stop short of the full training of the truth, to rest satisfied in a half-conversion, and shut his eyes to the superior claims of Christ over the teachers of human wisdom, to the special doctrines He has revealed, the special objects for which He has built His Church, for which He has made it so strong and enduring that the 'gates of Hell'—all the power of evil and of falsehood—shall not ultimately prevail against it.

And accordingly from the first the Christian Church was put on its guard against it. The mass of the believers had no sympathy with the refinements of the Schools: doctors sprang up among them, jealous of any appeal to the principles of antiquity, determined to claim for the Gospel its own witness to itself, and to dissever it entirely from the past. Of such a school of apology the impetuous Tertullian is the fittest representative, and following immediately upon Justin and Clement, he thus distinctly impeaches and repudiates their teaching :—

'Some of our brethren,' he says, 'who have persisted in the cultivation of letters, and have preserved faithfully in their recollection their old Pagan learning, have composed treatises expressly to convince us that there is nothing new, nothing extraordinary, in our religion; that the Gospel is founded, after all, on the common consent of humanity, and has only improved, exalted, and ratified the discoveries of antiquity. But what have these discoveries done for Christ? What hearts have they softened? What passions have they controlled? To such teaching men may listen while it appeals to the intellect only: as soon as it lays claim to the heart they fly back to their idols again. The labour, then, is lost. A man may spend his life in ransacking the stores of human wisdom, and may fail altogether of the true end of preaching, the bringing souls to Christ.' The argument then is delusive; whether sound or not, it is of no practical value :—such seems to be the writer's reasoning. Let us try, he would say, some other method more effectual.

'If we cannot persuade men by Heathen testimony, can we hope to do so by our own Christian Scriptures? True though they be, will they practically serve our turn? Will the Pagan listen to them? He is too proud, too vain of his own learning, too confident in his own masters. The Scriptures! none come to the Scriptures but Christians. You cannot attack the Pagan in his strongholds by the words of Christ. Scripture is the instrument of Christians in controversy among themselves: with Scripture we train the young believer, we reclaim the disobedient, we chastise the reprobate, we confute the erring; we deal in many ways with those who acknowledge their authority, even if they dispute their meaning or application. But with the Pagan, who admits not their divine character, you must go to work in none of these ways. You must appeal, then, to the Conscience:—the spontaneous witness of the human soul proclaims the truth of Christ.' It is to the heart, to the Conscience, that Tertullian appeals for an answer to those who examine him concerning the grounds of his faith. The Conscience, he declares, is *naturally Christian*.

Stand forth then, O soul, O Conscience of man,—whether we should acknowledge you to be eternal and divine, and therefore the more incapable of deceiving and betraying us;—or whether, as some indeed maintain, you have received no promise of immortality, and may therefore speak more independently, more fearlessly:—whether you descend from heaven; whether you issue from the earth; whether formed of members or of atoms; whether born with the body, or pre-existent to it:—you are still equally the seat of reason, of intelligence, and of feeling. I invoke you, not as you are polished and matured in schools and libraries, redolent of ancient wisdom, of the Academy and of the Porch. I call upon you rather, simple, rude, ignorant, untutored, such as you are among the children of nature merely,—in the street, in the field, in the workshop. You are not Christian, I know;—for no man is *born* a Christian—we must be *made* Christians. Nevertheless we Christians invoke your testimony, although you be not yet of our sect. You shall witness for us, and against your own fellows. You shall shame them! You shall convert them!'

But what are the Christian truths precisely to which Tertullian invokes the testimony of the universal conscience? The object, be it remembered, of the apologist of that day was not altogether the same as ours might be. It was first and chiefly to recall the heathen from their false and mean ideas of the Godhead; from polytheism; from idolatry. The overthrow of the idols was to be the foundation of Christian teaching; the establishment of a pure and reasonable Theism; the acknowledgment of a God of holiness and truth, of justice and mercy; a Punisher and a Rewarder. The great doctrines of the Gospel, in the eyes of that age, were assuredly the Resurrection and a future Life. It is to these cardinal truths, then, that the testimony of the soul is produced. The Heathen is shown that he is naturally not worse but better than his creed; that his notion of God, attested by a thousand involuntary admissions, is purer; that his hope of the future, gleaming in a thousand natural acts and utterances, is more consolatory; that his confidence in a superior Providence is more intimate and effectual. He is led to own that he is not really a believer in the frivolous fancies of men, to which he has been wont outwardly to conform himself, but that against many of the gross and hateful inventions of the flesh his reason, give it but room and play, will naturally revolt.

'These testimonies,' exclaims the apologist, 'are all the more true, because they are simple; all the more simple, because they are popular; the more popular inasmuch as they are universal; the more universal, as being natural; the more natural, as being divine.' 'Natural they are, and original in the soul. Say not that they have been derived from book-learning. The soul is older than any book: thought is older than eloquence: man was before the philosopher and the prophet.'

If we were now, in our day, to follow out the line of argument from the testimony of the soul, we should doubtless extend it far beyond its witness to the Unity, the Providence, the first attributes of God, and the promise of a future Resurrection. We should speak, and, even more strongly, of its conviction that sin is a reality, that forgiveness is necessary, that human merits are a delusion, that man requires a Mediator and a Redeemer. We should appeal to Conscience for its testimony against ourselves, against our acts, our thoughts, our natural corruption. We should point historically to the tokens it has given of this sense of sin, in the yearning of man for a sacrifice, a sufficient expiation, and in the innumerable inventions by which he has sought to realize it. The Cross of Christ would stand out in bold relief as the one intelligible and satisfying phenomenon, which millions among us have recognized as the thing they especially longed for in their ignorance and darkness,—as the sign to which the believer clings in faith, to which he bows in humility, which responds to his wants, and comforts him in his despondency. And further, we should present the divine person of the Holy Spirit as the full complement to that of Christ,—as the Comforter, the Counsellor, the Sanctifier, who leads us to Christ, and makes his cross available for our salvation.

All this, we should say, is the witness of the conscience naturally Christian. The truth of the whole cycle of saving doctrine is attested by the testimony of the heart. We could not be satisfied with less. The apologist of the third century stopped far short of this. But why? He left the deeper and the remoter doctrines of the Gospel for the most part to the teaching of the church services,—in which they may be traced from the fragments of her liturgies, communicated as they were gradually and methodically to her advancing disciples. It was in the sacraments of the Church rather than in the apologies of her champions, in her inner teaching of her own children rather than in her outward addresses to the Heathen, that the full import of the Christian sacrifice was set forth, under the invocation of the Holy Spirit. It is thus, I believe, that much which seems imperfect in the polemics of Tertullian may be truly and sufficiently explained.

The same doctor, it has been said, lays little direct

stress upon the historic truth of the facts recorded in the Scriptures of the New Testament. He tells us himself that such an appeal would not have answered his purpose. The Heathen would not have listened to it. He must work with the materials before him. He must direct himself to objects within his reach. We must not quarrel with his mode of operation. We may be sure that he knew his own business. The fact is that in his age the Pagans were not yet sufficiently moved by the progress of the new opinions to concern themselves with their outward credentials. But the time was at hand for a more direct demonstration of the Faith. The first direct assertion of the historic truth of our records is that of Origen, a generation after Tertullian, in refuting the objections urged by Celsus. The objector was himself a Pagan philosopher; but he was conversant with the polemics of Judaism, and from them no doubt he learned—what he would hardly have learned from purely Pagan sources—the mode in which the fortress of Christianity, her historic position, could be most plausibly assailed. Accordingly in his attack upon the veracity of the Gospels he assumes generally the mask of a Jew. The Jews, he knows, have from the first contested the truth of the Christian records. From the first they have asserted, for instance, that the disciples came by night and stole the body of Jesus. Such questions the Heathen have hitherto scornfully disregarded. They would not condescend to argue 'what is Truth' with the upstart sectarians. But the Heathen is beginning to get curious about it now. He sees patent before him the engrossing fact of the success of this 'illicit religion.' He can no longer put it by. He may assail it again and again with violence and persecution, but, somehow or other, this mode of refutation no longer satisfies him as of yore. It is plainly inconclusive. It has not gained its end. He begins to fear that it never will gain its end. His conscience demands to be set at rest about it. His judgment requires to be fortified against this importunate novelty. He asks himself, 'How have the Jews done with regard to it? They are more nearly concerned with it than we are. Let us follow their footsteps, and trace their arguments—under disguise at first—for we are still half-ashamed of entering into controversy with the foe we have been wont to burn and crucify.'

Accordingly, Celsus assuming the mask of a Jewish doctor, goes thoroughly into the question of the historic credibility of the Gospels. He brings to his task the stores, no doubt, of earlier controversy; his arguments are the ripened fruit of a full century of Jewish polemics. They are full, comprehensive, shrewd, ingenious. They combine, it is said, almost all the points of objection which have been raised in repeated succession in later times. They fix themselves on the weak points, on all the apparent inconsistencies or discrepancies of the four converging narratives; they hit every reputed blot as unerringly as the shafts of the most practised of the moderns. Celsus was assuredly no beginner in such a mode of warfare; he was no sciolist in the art of controversy. Such an assailant was not to be contemned. His attack must be met and rebutted triumphantly. The foundations of the Church were imperilled in the face of the world. The whole array of Jewish and Heathen antagonists was standing tiptoe in expectation, at a combat which was no longer carried on in the obscure schools of oppressed and cowering Judaism, but had become the common quarrel of mankind.

The new assault required a new system of defence.

The method employed by Origen, a worthy champion at so momentous a crisis, was to show that the records of the Christian Revelation do bear the seal of historic fact. With the first objections of the Hebraic disputant, those directed against the character and condition of the Messiah—his lowliness, his weakness, the fact of his death of ignominy—we have little concern. The objection is Jewish; at least it is obsolete. It is met by the higher and nobler view of the ends of Revelation familiar to every Christian. The story thus objected to is shown to be consistent with the methods of Divine Providence, to be analogous to the circumstances which no less attended the ministry even of many Pagan teachers of acknowledged wisdom and holiness. But, what is more important for us, this line of argument leads to the direct assertion of the personality of the Saviour; it requires a constant reference to the historical data of the Scriptures; it asserts the veracity of the writers of the sacred records; it meets the objections from their pretended inconsistencies; it brings into prominent relief the full and constant conviction of the early disciples, of the men who had the nearest and most intimate knowledge of all the circumstances, and who would have been the last to pin their faith, even unto death, upon fables cunningly devised or carelessly accepted. It shows how many statements of fact, which to us may seem questionable or unintelligible, were readily accepted by both the believers and their adversaries, in the age which could most justly appreciate the circumstances. At least, if we still, in the pride of our presumed advance in critical sagacity, demur to the grounds of primitive belief and acknowledgment, it proves beyond dispute that the records we now possess are precisely the same that lay open to Celsus and to Origen, and, as we may fairly presume, to some generations before them. It establishes the continuity of the Faith, and brings us face to face with almost the first epoch of discussion on the subject. Christianity, we learn from it, has been in its main features, as established by its historical documents, one and the same for sixteen, nay, for eighteen centuries.

And perhaps we shall feel the better disposed towards the evidence of Christian truth as maintained by the genius of Origen, when we observe how secondary is the place, after all, which he assigns to the testimony of miracles. Origen, at least, is not to be charged with hasty illogical deference to the superstitions of an unscientific age. While maintaining the actual truth of the miraculous narratives of the Gospels, he lays little stress upon them to establish the truth of the Christian Revelation. He believes assuredly in God's power and will to change, for adequate purposes, the appointed course of nature; but he would not regard any apparent or actual miracle as a proof of divine interference, apart from the attestation of a moral doctrine. Man alone—the heart and conscience of man—can judge of the fitness of the occasion, and therewith of the divine authority of the miracle. But the works of Jesus Christ do all approve themselves to the enlightened conscience of His creatures. Such signs could not have been effected by a power antagonist to God; from God they must spring, and from God only. The doctrine of the Saviour, full of love and grace, was worthy that such things should be done for it. It reveals salvation not to the wise and prudent only, after the fashion of human philosophy; it addresses the child, the woman, the slave, and the ignorant. It invites all who thirst to drink of the water of eternal life. It awakens in every bosom the sense of its likeness to God, in whose image every man was created. It treats with respect, with reverential care, this image of God in the soul of man, however fallen from its high estate. Thus it justifies and explains the great mystery of Revelation, the self-abasement of the Mighty One, the sufferings and the death of God incarnate. And, finally, it is not ashamed of Christ crucified; it blushes not for the Son of God extended on the accursed tree for the souls of the children of God.

And this it is which leads the great apologist to dwell

with especial force and emphasis on the fact and meaning of the crucifixion. It is established by history, it is explained by theology. It is God teaching by example. Origen regards the Crucifixion as the moral key to the Gospel Revelation, as the explanation of God's dispensation to this latter age. He maintains the exact truth of the sacred narrative against the sneers of the Jew and the scruples of the Pagan. For the Crucifixion, in his eyes, is Christianity itself. The great value of the apology of Origen, full as it is of learning and of feeling, consists in the decisive stand it makes for the personality of the Lord Jesus, and for the actual certainty of the records of His ministry. This is its character, its principle, as compared with the apologies which have preceded it. It introduces us to a new phase of the mighty controversy; a phase which has been presented to many a generation afterwards, but which first assumed its distinctive importance in the age of the teacher before us. And the answer which we shall make to men that do examine us must still be in principle his: some of his positions may be insecure, some of his weapons may be obsolete; but the fortress he seized is still the stronghold of Christianity: we will hold it and defend it for ever.

But Origen is a man of wide and liberal sympathies. He does not confine himself within the lines of the apology from history. Again and again he falls back on the generous theories of his predecessors; he gathers new strength from contact with the teaching of Justin and

Clement. He, too, presents to us the incarnate Son of God as the Word revealed to the philosophers, as the Desired of all nations, yearned and hoped for by every pure and tender spirit among men. But to discern His beauty and divinity beneath the veil of His humiliation, we must have a new sense—the new eye of a purified understanding; we must break with sin, raise ourselves above the soil and dust of this lower world, even to the heights of celestial purity, beyond the taint of worldly sin and corruption. Those only shall see and believe who shall wish to see and to profit. This is the feeling which Origen seeks to awaken in the mind of his opponent, whether he be Jew or Greek. This he entreats, he urges, he adjures him to entertain. To this end he conducts the discussion, and makes every argument lead to this. He preaches faith. He asserts that faith is to be attained by all who sincerely do the will of God: 'He that doeth the will of God shall know of the doctrine.' Thus he reconciles respect for human nature with hatred of sin which has corrupted it. His reasoning all tends to a moral end. Oppressed with a sense of the awful corruption of the age around him, full of the spirit of the divine Master whom he serves, he feels how worthy the Gospel is to reform mankind, to purify human nature, to lead to God, and finally, through His grace, to join unto God. This union with God is the end of all his preaching, the completion of his aspirations and desires. It is the end, he believes, of Christ's mission upon earth. To this all things, in his system, tend; without this, completed and perfected, the dispensation of the Saviour would, he conceives, be frustrated. His ardour leads him perhaps beyond his warrant. His enthusiasm overleaps the bounds which a tamer and more cautious interpretation of Scripture has imposed upon the Church. He believes in the ultimate reconciliation of all men, of every soul of men, and of devils also, to God—for so widely, so fancifully, does he interpret the promised restitution of all things. He quits the sure path of Scripture, and wanders in the mazes of the philosophers. If this be an error in fact—as, certainly, it exceeds the limits of the revealed—it is, at least, a generous error. If it be a heresy, it is one which has found, and is likely, perhaps, to find, few followers. If it is too bold, there are few, perhaps, who will have the courage to embrace it. But the Church of God is a jealous Church, and to the Church it savoured of Paganism; it augured that reaction of vain human imaginations, which was even then impending, against which it was the sacred mission of the Church to guard. To that jealous apprehension of Paganism—above, below, on every side, watching at every aperture for an entrance, ever attacking and ever to be repulsed—we owe all our safety. And Paganism has not been extinguished, and never will be extinguished, in the self-willed indiscipline of the human heart; least of all, as will presently appear, was it extinguished in the great age of Pagan reaction, the fourth and fifth centuries of our era.[1]

[1] Notes and Illustrations (A).

LECTURE III.

DOGMATIC INFERENCES FROM CHRIST'S REVELATION: ATHANASIUS AND AUGUSTINE.

COLOSS. II. 8, 9, 10.

Beware lest any man spoil you through philosophy and vain deceit, after the tradition of men, after the rudiments of the world, and not after Christ.
For in him dwelleth all the fulness of the Godhead bodily.
And ye are complete in Him.

THIS text is important for the purpose of these lectures, at the point at which we have now arrived. It declares, in conformity with the whole tenor of the epistle from which it is taken, that Scripture reveals the nature of the Godhead, as of something beyond the power of human intellect to discover, as God's discovery of Himself to His creatures; and at the same time it discloses to us that which is equally beyond our means of discovering for ourselves, the relation in which man stands to God, and the foundation of his duties towards the great Author of his being. But it further declares to us that the traditions of men, the rudiments of the world, the imaginations, the learning, the religions, and the philosophies of the Heathen, are ever prone to place themselves in opposition to these doctrinal discoveries, to contend against them, to draw men away from them, and indispose them to the reception of the truth as it is in Christ Jesus. It announces the solemn truth that Revelation is a Theology, and that the natural man ever rebels against its theological teaching, and is ever falling away to conceits and inventions of his own. It reminds the Colossians, to whom it is addressed, and us unto whom its echoes have descended, of the fervent invitation before made by the apostle, to acknowledge—for love, for comfort, for understanding—the mystery of God, and of the Father, and of Christ, in whom are hid all the treasures of wisdom and of knowledge. And this more particularly, considering the danger in which all men actually lie, of 'being beguiled with enticing words,' of being made subject again to mere Pagan imaginations from which, by God's blessing, we have been freed, of being ensnared by human appetites and temptations, 'for which things the wrath of God cometh on the children of disobedience.'

The text, I say, is important at the present stage of our discussion; for we are now arrived at an era of dogmatic teaching, of the formal establishment of the Christian theology, of the technical statement of the nature of God, and the relation of man to Him. The Fourth Century, or the Nicene period, is marked by the most direct and formal definition on these two cardinal points of revealed religion; by the determination of the real creed of the Church on the questions raised by the heresy of Arius on the one hand, and on the other by the heresy of Pelagius. The Fourth Century places the religion of Christ definitively on the basis of a revealed Theology, which it has since held, which has been consistently maintained as its great characteristic, in which it stands wholly apart and distinct from the pretended revelations or mythologies of the Pagan world; which is, we believe, the real pledge and charter of its authority over the human conscience, the seal of its divinity, the secret of its power, the principle of its life and immortality: 'even the mystery which hath been hid from ages and from generations, but now is made manifest unto His saints.'[1]

Now this assertion of dogma, as the living principle of Christianity, could not have been maintained without a previous assertion of the historic truth of the records on which it is founded. The teaching of Athanasius and Augustine, of Ambrose and Basil, Gregory and Jerome, who all belong to the same school of complete Christian theology, could not have been promulgated, had not Origen gone before, and brought prominently forward, as I lately showed, the divine authority of the written Word. The Apology against Celsus, which we considered at our last meeting, is the basis of the Athanasian and of Augustinian theology. It establishes a published and recognised Text, an open Bible, as the accredited ground of appeal on all hands, as a firm foothold and

[1] Coloss. i. 26.

handhold for the professed theologian, for the man of spiritual science, the deductive reasoner from the word spoken to the Word who speaketh. As long as the distinct claims of our sacred records to the belief and allegiance of Christians were postponed to speculative considerations, to the external argument from their fulfilment of human auguries and imaginations, advanced by Justin and by Clement, there was no ground prepared for the carefel textual investigation of the nature of God the Son, once apparent in the flesh, as revealed in Holy Scripture. Accordingly, the utterances of the earlier Fathers on this mysterious subject were fewer, less distinct, less uniform and consistent. There was as yet no technical language on the subject; the age had not required it, and no one had been impelled by the pressure of demand to offer it. The Church, in its corporate capacity, had been content with its implicit belief, shadowed forth in prayers and rituals, not embodied in dogmatic treatises. But in the third century, the polemics of Origen more especially brought the importance of the written Word, of the letter of Scripture, more prominently into view; and when, in the age succeeding, circumstances led to a full and anxious appreciation of the texts relating to Christ's divinity, the way had been prepared, the Church was not sleeping in her temples, or muttering senseless liturgies, but could speak the thoughts which were in her, imbued with the deepfelt teaching of her immemorial traditions.

And these circumstances—what were they? Why

did the question of dogma assume such special importance just at this moment?

When, some time ago, I was describing the meeting of the Christian Fathers at the famous council of Nicæa, I dropped incidentally the statement, that many of the Heathens, philosophers and inquirers, hovered about the appointed place of meeting, and evinced both curiosity and interest in the question to be debated. The mention was by the way, but it was not without a purpose. This prying of the Pagans into the mysterious dogmas of the Gospel was a fruitful incident; fruitful, not only of conversion and belief among the Pagans, but of the formal establishment of Christian doctrine itself, and therewith of the permanent duration and fullest extension of Christ's kingdom also; fruitful however, also, of much internal error and dissension, of schism and persecution, of the loss of souls as well as of the gain of souls, of corruption and death as well as of truth and salvation.

For, in fact, the views of Arius, which gave occasion to the meeting of the Nicene council, indicated something more than a difference of opinion among Christians. They were really the embodiment, under conditions of Christian thought, of a germ of Pagan feeling, of which the heretic himself was very possibly unconscious. But his eyes might indeed have been opened to it even by the interest which the Pagans so manifestly took in the question he had launched into discussion.

Arius might well have applied to himself the words I have cited from the apostle: 'Beware lest any man spoil you through philosophy and vain deceit, after the tradition of men, after the rudiments of the world, and not after Christ.' St. Paul had gone on to say: 'For in Him dwelleth all the fulness of the Godhead bodily.' And when the heretic felt, as he must have felt, the plain incongruity, to say the least, of this last assertion with his own lower views of the person of the Saviour, he might have remembered that such notions as his were precisely those which best accorded with the Pagan inventions, with that descending scale of the divine hierarchy which obtained more or less distinctly in every popular mythology, in every transcendental theosophy, from the Ganges to the Tiber.

The distinctions, indeed, which Arius and his party drew between their views and the extreme theories of the Humanitarian Paulus are not undeserving of regard. No doubt Christ's divinity was an article of their creed; and this divinity they enhanced by allowing His pre-existence to all the creation of God. Yet the Son Himself they affirmed to be a creature; His nature they considered inferior to that of the Father; His existence they maintained to have had no actual beginning; He was subject in their view Himself to actual moral probation; He was liable to sin, adopted only on proof of His worthiness; the Logos or Word they held to be an attribute of the one God shown forth in the Son as a creature.

The principle which underlies all these notions is precisely such as would recommend itself to a Pagan theologian—the essential inferiority of Christ to God. This principle once admitted would cover the Pagan's conception of all the lower deities of the Olympian synod, of the demigods whom labours and sufferings had raised to heavenly thrones; of heroes and good men made perfect, and exalted to be benefactors of their species in a higher place and with a wider sphere of power. Arianism, then, was a slightly disguised Paganism: it sprang from the same recesses of the heart; and as such accordingly the shrewd Athanasius himself expressly denounced it.

Of this Arius may have been himself unconscious; even when advised and warned of it, he may have resisted or parried the conviction; but that the Pagans on their part were aware of it we cannot reasonably doubt. The Pagans who hovered about the council-hall of Nicæa, or listened on the threshold to the discussions of the fathers, were well assured that the battle to be fought was in fact their own battle; that the denounced of the Church was their own champion; that on the sentence of that day depended the definitive triumph of the new Theology and the extinction of the old-world idolatries; or whether—in some new phase, under some thin disguise, with the acceptance perhaps of a Christianizing phraseology—the conceptions of the human heart, the traditions of men, the rudiments of the world, should reassert their everlasting dominion, and conquered Greece once more make conquest of her conquerors. It was not merely a question of words, such as 'same' and 'similar;' not a question of a letter, of a single iota, as has been so petulantly asserted; but the question of Christianity or Paganism. Such was the issue in debate; and the issue was turned to the Christian side by the firm assertion of a doctrine founded upon such texts as this before us: 'In Him dwelleth all the fulness of the Godhead bodily.'

The controversy at Nicæa was indeed, outwardly and in the eye of the multitude, a civil war between contending parties in the Church; but it was not a 'war without a triumph,' for it was actually and implicity a struggle between Christianity and its foreign enemy; and that enemy it utterly routed by the blow which struck down for a time the false brother Arius.

For a time, I say; for a reverse of fortune was permitted, as you know, to follow, and Arius had again his hour of success and victory; the Pagans pursued his triumph, and shared his favouring gale; and we shall see how deep and deadly a wound they were able, rising ever with his rebound, to inflict at no distant time on the body of the Christian Church. So closely were the Pagans and the heretics bound up together: so truly was the cause of the one the cause of the other; so plainly did the same root of error lie at the bottom of both perversions of the truth; so necessary was then, as now, the assertion of catholic truth to keep out Paganism from the fold as well as to keep out heresy. The traditions of men and the rudiments of the world are ever sprouting afresh in the vineyard of Christ. The doctrine of God's fulness dwelling bodily in the man Jesus, though many disregard it as a vain imagination, is the legitimate deduction from Scripture.

But the text goes on to proclaim to the true disciples, 'And ye are complete in Him.' Here is another and not less important side of divine Revelation, namely, the relation of man to God. Jesus Christ has come into the world to announce to man the position in which he naturally stands to the Deity; the state of imperfection, corruption, reprobation, into which he has fallen; and the means divinely provided for recovering him from that state, restoring him to favour with God, making him acceptable to his Creator, and complete for the end and purpose of his creation: that is, for his reunion with the Divine, from which he seemed hopelessly separated. This is the Christian idea of religion; quite different from that of the Heathen world; quite different from that conceit of personal merit, and personal sufficiency, which lay at the root of the Pagan superstitions, and colours every deviation from the catholic doctrine of the Divine Nature; which is constantly recurring even among us, even among those who have been baptized and bred in the true faith of the Holy Trinity; so natural and congenial is it to the traditions of men, and the rudiments of the world within us.

The Apology of Origen had set forth the merit of Jesus Christ as our blessed Redeemer, and had placed in strong relief this great doctrine of Revelation, the completion of man by the act, not of his own virtue, but of God his Saviour—in short, the doctrine of Grace. That illustrious teacher had laid the foundation of belief not only in the relation of Jesus to God, as of one in whom dwelleth all the fulness of the Godhead bodily; but also in the relation of man to God, as requiring the sacrifice of Christ for his redemption, and sanctification through grace for his completion and acceptance. But the lines thus broadly drawn by Origen in these different directions were followed in the next age by two Christian doctors—the first almost exclusively by the one, the second more particularly by the other. Athanasius, as we have seen, fixed an unremitted glance on the revelations we have received of the nature of God and of Christ: Augustine, one generation later, could allow himself to dwell more emphatically on the nature of man in relation to God, and on the divine method, revealed in Scripture, of his spiritual renovation and completion. Augustine, indeed, in his manifold writings runs over the whole surface of the Christian Theology. His works are in themselves an encyclopædia of Theology. His books on the Trinity, for instance, are hardly less complete, searching, scientific, than those of Athanasius himself, whose attention to that one theme was almost undivided. Nevertheless, if we consider what was the great work of Augustine in the Church, we should say, I suppose, to establish the doctrine of human corruption, of original sin, and the need of grace divine to heal him, and to restore him to divine favour. Of all his controversies with the errors of his times none is so marked, none was so important in his own day, none has been since, and still is, and ever will be so important in respect of the eternal conflict of Christianity with our natural Paganism, as that with Pelagius, and with his assertion of man's sufficiency to work out his own salvation by his own merits, his own righteousness.

In the heresy of Arius we have traced the secret root of Paganism still working in the soil of the human heart, even among professed believers in the Gospel. And again in the heresy of Pelagius we may recognise the same restless activity of our inbred Paganism. In both lay the same implicit assurance of the sufficiency of human nature to raise itself up to God; to receive of the fulness of the Godhead; to become complete in Him here or hereafter. The Pagan mythologies declared that the best and wisest among men had been taken up into heaven, and there endowed with power apportioned to their wisdom and goodness—had become themselves Gods—Gods of an inferior caste, perhaps, demigods or demons; and such might be the case again, such was constantly the case—from Hercules it was but a step to Romulus, from Romulus to Augustus, from Augustus to the Cæsar, the prophet, or the favourite of the hour. Again, the Pagan philosophers, if they rejected this extravagance, still held and taught that man had in him every element of perfection; that he could justify himself, sanctify himself, purify himself 'even as He is pure;' and earn from Him, whose eyes are too pure to behold iniquity, the fulness of His favour here, and possibly, in some select, some lucky cases, future beatitude elsewhere. The scheme of Arius played into the hands of the mythologists: the fancy of Pelagius flattered and confirmed the philosophers. Both the one and the other were the best allies of Paganism in the hour of her defeat and humiliation, in the hour of her intrigues to recover herself, in the hour when, controlled by law and forbidden the arm of flesh, she was striving by deceit and cajolery to regain her empire over minds—to turn the flank of Christianity whose front she dared not assail. How far the great doctors of the Church were at the moment aware of this; how far they practically felt that in striking down Arius or Pelagius they were baffling the pontiffs and the Sophists, we need not curiously inquire. Possibly they were too fully engrossed with the object immediately before them to look through it and beyond it to the influences in the back-ground, to fond traditions of the heart, and visionary ideas of the understanding. But, if it were so, the fact would be none the less certain. From our more distant point of view we can clearly see the real upshot of the contest they had in hand, and recognise the Providence which at that crisis of spiritual religion raised a barrier against Paganism in the genuine deductions from Scripture of the Church and her doctors.

While, indeed, we acknowledge in Athanasius and Augustine two of the greatest champions of Christian theology in the contest with heathen naturalism, we may remark a difference, not unfruitful of results, in the temper of the men themselves, and in the completeness of their reasonings. The sobriety and self-restraint of Athanasius stand in marked contrast to the impetuousness, the ardour, the exaggerating spirit of Augustine. The aim of Athanasius is simple and limited. It is to establish the fulness of the Godhead in Christ; to show that the Son of God is Himself God in the highest sense —equal with the Father—born from all eternity, existing to all eternity—coequal, coeternal. These were the points at which his opponents faltered, on which they equivocated or wavered. They lowered the dignity of the Saviour, and therewith the importance of salvation. The controversialist might be tempted to dwell too exclusively on the distinctness of the Second Person, to forget the obligation to identify Him with the First, or again to insist upon the Trinity in disregard of the Unity, to subordinate faith to logic, revelation to understanding.

The greatness of Athanasius lay, it would seem, in the perfect self-command which enabled him to retain his grasp of his argument by both its handles; neither to confuse the persons, nor divide the substance; not to suffer his opponent to draw or drive him into untenable extremes, to tempt him to a spiritual defeat by the prospect of a triumph in logic. Great as Augustine was, he had not this greatness. The fiery African sometimes launched his javelin beyond recall. He was overmastered sometimes by his own powers of logic, perhaps of rhetoric. His victory was assured, but he carried it too far; and in overthrowing the Pagan doctrines of human merit and human sufficiency, the errors of Pelagius, he was borne away to the unqualified, uncompromising enunciation of the total corruption and utter helplessness of man; to the denial of all free-will and free agency, and implicitly of all moral responsibility, under an absolute predestination to salvation or perdition. He contemplated the utter ruin of all created being in the sin of Adam; not because all have sinned in the weakness of the flesh derived from Adam, but in and for the sin of Adam himself; a doctrine very fearful in its theoretical aspect—in the dismay with which it must affect us, ignorant as we must be of our lot from all time predestined; in the excess of recklessness or of presumption to which it may impel us; but which has been found more fearful still in its practical consequences, in setting the duty of bringing souls into covenant with God above every moral consideration, of converting and baptizing by force or fraud, by persecuting or by lying; of *compelling men* to come in by the sword of the magistrate. It gives a terribly literal emphasis to the expression of Scripture on the peril of the unbeliever, of the ignorant, of the unconscious and the infant. It throws a dark shadow over human nature, and aggravates every moral evil which it proposes to exterminate. It destroys bodies which are not its own to deal with, for the shadow of a chance of saving souls which are none but God's only.

The doctrine of Predestination urged too logically by

Augustine against the overweening logic of the naturalist Pelagius, has been, it is too true, the parent of dreadful horrors; it would have worked even worse harm among us but for the common-sense and feeling of mankind, which has practically denied its legitimate consequences, or more commonly perhaps supplied, tacitly and unconsciously, the necessary corrective.

For as in the nature of the Divine Being as revealed to our apprehensions, there is a logical contradiction which Faith must acknowledge and allow for; as Christ upon earth was man, and at the same time was God also; as Christ in heaven is One with the Father and yet distinct in person from the Father,—so in the relation of Man to God there is also an inconsistency to be admitted. An insoluble problem is enunciated to us: to prove the coexistence of Grace with Merit, to reconcile the fact of Free-will with the theory of Necessity. There is text to be marshalled against text, reason to be confronted with reason; the mystery of the Man-God is renewed in every soul that is born into the world; in each of us dwells a human element combined with a divine influence. The Gospel, which is the revelation of the Man-God, preaches also the religion of Grace and of Free-will. It presumes both the one and the other; it declares their coequal authority. It presents to us salvation as the decree of the Almighty, and the sovereign act of His love; as an act of pardon, of reconciliation to Himself, springing from His gracious favour, effected through His Son, His well-beloved, by a mysterious sacrifice of unimaginable worthiness, attended with the effluence of His sanctifying Spirit. It is not we that have chosen Him, sought Him, supplicated Him; but He that hath chosen us, come forth from the recesses of His being to solicit us. All grace, like every other perfect gift, comes down from Him who is the Father of Light. Very true: yet this same Gospel, which thus signalizes the character of Grace, does no less presume and demonstrate our Free-will; does no less appeal to us, by our own power and energy to meet Grace and receive it, to open our hearts to entertain the Saviour, and of our own consent give harbour to the Sanctifier. We must *come* to Him if we would be saved, we must *strive* for Him, we must *knock*, we must *run* as in a race, we must *take* up our cross and *follow* Him. We must have Faith, and do the works of Faith; we must live a life in His service, though we cannot see or feel or handle Him. In short, the Gospel will not suffer us to regard ourselves as altogether absorbed in God, and as having no position external to Him. It will not let us abandon ourselves to Mysticism, to Quietism, to Pantheism. It will not surrender us to the Oriental heathenisms against which it bore emphatic testimony from the beginning. Now Pelagius, a teacher from the West, regarded man—with the western Pagans, with the Greeks and the Romans, the Celts and the Teutons—as too remote from God, too independent of His influences. Augustine, leaning unwarily to the Eastern enthusiasts, to the dreams of Gnostics and of Brahmins, fell into the opposite extravagance;

he was led further and further in the ardour of discussion, to see in man the mere effluence of God, with no independence of his own at all. True religion, not snapped from a text here or a chapter there, but gathered together from the full comparison of all its teaching—from balancing Paul with John, and James, and Peter, and holding Christ and His utterances supreme over all —has maintained from the first its equal measure, and enthroned a theory distinct from the extremes both of the Eastern and the Western Theosophies.[1]

The bearing of what has been now said will be seen perhaps more clearly on a future occasion, when we shall examine the reaction from Christian dogma which characterized in many quarters the age which next succeeded. For such, it may be thought, was the penalty exacted of the Church for the triumph she too easily accorded to the doctrinal exaggerations of Augustine.

Nevertheless we must not fail at this point to remark how the extremes of theoretical teaching have generally been tempered in practice by the sobering and sanctifying influence of Christian culture. Both the Pelagian view and the Augustinian of Grace and Free-will, have had their patrons and disciples among wise and good men in all ages. Both have been favoured with recognition by schools and councils in the Church. Men, it has been said, are never so bad as their opinions; the actions of good men can hardly be so wrong as are often their arguments. Christians, we may truly assert, are

[1] Notes and Illustrations (B).

never wholly unchristianized by their doctrinal eccentricities. Of the noble Augustine we may say at least, that no Christian teacher has ever laboured more sedulously, none perhaps more effectually, to build up a lofty Christian morality, in spite of a doctrine which would seem logically to undermine and utterly subvert it. The consciousness present to him of the actual mass of sin around him—sin among the heathens, sin hardly less gross and rampant among the Christians, sin in the court, in the council, and in the market-place—overcame all his theories, and impelled him to spend and be spent in the service of godly morality. The time was coming, as he perhaps himself anticipated, when the flood of human corruption would overflow all its banks, and the world of culture and religion seem about to perish in the inundation. Against this second Deluge he contended bravely to the end, with his eyes ever fixed upon the rainbow of promise; and fruitless as his efforts may appear at the time—for the flood came, though God with His own hand arrested it—he has left to after-ages, to more hopeful ages, to our own age, a store of exhortation, of precept, of counsel, which has surely in all generations made many wise unto salvation. He has been himself for fifteen centuries the salt of Christian divinity; every fresh revival of religion among us has drawn strength from descending into his medicinal waters; and multitudes, we doubt not, in every Christian country have been made, through his preaching, complete in Christ their Saviour.[1]

[1] Notes and Illustrations (C).

LECTURE IV.

RELAPSE OF CHRISTIAN BELIEF AND PRACTICE.

1 Samuel ii. 12.

They knew not the Lord.

I have set before you in the preceding lectures the teaching of the doctors of the early Church in its most prominent feature—namely, the recommendation of Christian doctrine to the Pagan world. Justin and Clement, Tertullian and Origen, Athanasius and Augustine have passed successively before you: the apologies for Christianity have gradually widened their base, and the structure which has been raised upon them presents to us the full front of our Lord's dogmatic teaching; the revelation made by Him of the nature of God, and man's relation to Him.

Christian Theology has been expanded before us, the economy of grace, the covenant of mercy, the theory of Justification and Redemption in Christ Jesus the Son of God the Father. This transcendental teaching culminated in the simple declaration that to know God and to see God is to do His commandments:—that our salvation is to be worked out by each of us with the assistance of the Spirit:—that pure morality lies at the root of the true Christian life.

From a foundation thus fitly laid what blessed issues might be expected! The promise of Christendom had been fair and full of encouragement, and the labour of the husbandman had not been wanting to cherish the divine plant. The age of the persecutions and martyrdoms, the age of sowing and watering, had brought forth abundantly. The lives of Christians had been the most effective argument for the truth of their doctrine. By this evidence among others, possibly beyond all others, had the triumph of the Gospel been attained—that outward success which we exalt, speaking humanly, with the name of a triumph—though while we use the word, and utter the felicitations it implies, we may ask ourselves with a sigh, Has the success been inward and spiritual after all? Has the worldly triumph been a triumph in God's eyes? Has the Church, clothed in purple, crowned with the mitre, enthroned in palaces and temples, seated at the right hand of emperors, armed with the sword to punish as well as with the sceptre to command, secured the spiritual objects of her mission? Have the kingdoms of this world as yet truly 'become the kingdoms of our Lord and of His Christ?'[1]

In the present discourse I wish to set before you some of the plainest facts which must tend to modify and chasten our estimation of this temporal triumph. I

[1] Rev. xi. 15.

wish to show how in the age of Athanasius and Augustine themselves, in the age which immediately followed the political recognition of the Christian Faith, there was a manifest decline in spiritual religion, a decay of spiritual life :—how the Church became in some respects an open apostate; how her love grew cold, her faith languid; Christianity faded away into colourless indifference: Paganism, latent or avowed, recovered no small portion of the ground she had recently surrendered; the dreams of human speculation enticed men from the firm foundations of revealed dogma :—how, finally, the time approached for the world to be smitten with the punishment of her backsliding, and the Church to be chastened with a long and terrible trial, from which indeed she has never yet emerged in her proper purity and power. Like the strong man Samson, her locks were shorn in penalty of her disobedience, and if her strength has grown again with her locks, the opportunity for its exercise has been lost; she has been chained to the forms and usages of the world, and served the passions and caprices of her mundane task-masters.

Such spiritual declines, with their appointed penalties, have occurred again and again in the course of God's dealings with His people. The Jewish Church was repeatedly smitten to the ground for disobedience, and raised again, but to a lesser share of favour and enlightenment, on its enforced repentance.

Take the instance to which our text refers, which

may serve in more than one particular to illustrate the crisis on which we are this day engaged :—

'The sons of Eli were sons of Belial: they knew not the Lord.' Eli, the judge and priest of Israel, was himself, it seems, not in the direct line of priestly succession. He was not of the house of Eleazar, the eldest son of Aaron, to which the succession was legitimately due. God had seen fit to transfer this prerogative, for ends not disclosed to us, from the chosen branch of the chosen family to another stock, the house of Ithamar. Again, Eli combined powers which had originally been kept separate in the polity of God's people. He was both Judge and Priest; he was chief political and spiritual. Eli had done good service in his youth; he had merited his advancement; he had distinguished himself in God's cause. But in old age he had lost his strength of character; his vices or weaknesses had gained dominion over him. Indolence in spiritual things, indulgence to worldly feelings, pride of place perhaps, and security in his Master's favour, had allowed him to think of his Master's business as if it were his own, to prostitute the sacred office to unworthy purposes, to fill the priests' places with the worldly and the worthless among men, to favour his own children at the expense of the people, and to the dishonour of God. The sons of Eli were sons of Belial; full of all manner of lewdness and corruption; turning the service of God into a lie; turning themselves into heathens, infidels, atheists, even in the inner temple and sanctuary of the Most High. And accordingly God prepared a terrible judgment. He brought the armed hosts of Philistia, the old inveterate enemies of Israel, to Aphek. He suffered His own chosen people to be overthrown and smitten before the Philistines. And when the people, stricken and dismayed, said, 'Let us fetch the ark of the covenant of the Lord out of Shiloh unto us, that, when it cometh among us, it may save us out of the hands of our enemies;' and when the sons of Eli the priests of God, Hophni and Phinehas, 'were there with the ark of the covenant of God,' and 'all Israel shouted with a great shout, so that the earth rang again;' —then the Philistines when they heard the shout were afraid, 'for they said, God is come into the camp. And they said, Woe unto us! for there hath not been such a thing heretofore. Woe unto us! who shall deliver us out of the hand of these mighty gods? these are the gods that smote the Egyptians with all the plagues in the wilderness. Be strong and quit yourselves like men.' And so Providence took their side, for its own divine purposes,—and 'the Philistines fought, and Israel was smitten,—and the ark of God was taken in Shiloh.' [1]

We need not go further. This special instance of man's provocation and God's rebuke, of the falling away of God's Church, and of its being smitten with a dire discomfiture, was repeated in the age which followed the political recognition and establishment of Christianity. The Church was enthroned at Rome as the ark had been laid up in Shiloh. In Eli, the chosen of God by special

[1] 1 Sam. iv. 3–9.

favour in place of the legitimate claimants to the priesthood, we may see the Christian Church, received into God's covenant in place of the Jewish. The judge-priest may represent to us that union of Church and State, that combination of the secular with the spiritual power, which marked this era in the Roman polity; a union not repudiated by God Himself, nay, rather allowed and sanctioned in the one case and in the other; but nevertheless a union fraught with peculiar dangers and temptations, exposed to excesses and corruptions; a union which, while it answered its purpose in fusing the manifold prejudices of the nations into one form of doctrine, did undoubtedly produce many internal evils, and issued in the glaring apostasy from spiritual Christianity so widely spread in the next generation. In the faithless sons of Eli we may notice the voluptuous vices, the flaunting sensuality, which disgraced the name of Christians in the court, in the temple, in private society; the corruption of the world, which loudly proclaimed itself no longer Pagan; vice and sin so gross, so open, as to cast suspicion on the truth of Christ, and drive men in despair from His service. 'Men abhorred the offerings of the Lord.' Men relapsed into Paganism or Atheism.

And lastly, the marshalling of the hosts of Philistia, the hereditary foes of Israel, may bring to mind the gathering of the barbarians on the frontiers of the empire; the renewal under other auspices of that ancient strife between the Germans and the Romans, now at last to be concluded with a great and irreversible victory. The trembling of the Philistines at the appearance of the ark in the camp of Israel may represent the alarm of the wild men of the North at the terror, widely bruited, of Christian portent and miracle. The 'Woe unto us, who shall deliver us out of the hands of these mighty gods?' comes back upon us with a wilder wail, in the voice of the proud Merovingian, stretched at last on his death-bed after fifty years of power:—'Wa! wa! who is this king in heaven, who thus slays at will the great ones of the earth?'[1]

Yet as the spot where the Philistines encountered the Israelites was known first by the name of Aphek, and afterwards by the happier title of Ebenezer, or the stone of help—for though vanquished then, the Israelites did on that same spot gain, through God's help, a victory later—so was this Aphek of the Christians succeeded by its Ebenezer also; the military triumph of the barbarians became in its appointed time the peaceful and spiritual triumph of the Church and of the Gospel. The Goths who entered Rome as Pagans or Arians, remained there Christians themselves and orthodox believers. God worked out His designs for the victory of His Truth in both cases. His hand had been still over the Israelites in the darkest hour of their defeats and captivities: His hand was no less extended to save and sustain the Church of His own Son, when Alaric entered Rome, and when Attila retired before His servant Leo.

What was really the proportion of professing Chris-

[1] Notes and Illustrations (D).

tians to the whole population of the Empire at the period before us, has never been ascertained, and may even baffle conjecture. In the West at least, and at Rome especially, the Pagans seem still to have retained a numerical preponderance; and though from the time of Theodosius, that is during the career of Augustine himself, the celebration of their rites was forbidden, their temples closed or overthrown, there was much covert Pagan service, much connived at, many superstitions commonly practised; the teaching of the Pagan philosophies was openly allowed; the schools were frequented; much learning and eloquence were employed in defence of old intellectual associations. The Senate of Rome was still the stronghold of the ancient traditions; and neither shame nor fear repressed the profession among numbers of every class, of some shadow at least of old Pagan belief.

But whatever may have been the relative proportion of the Christians and the Pagans at this period, there is ample evidence to show how great had been the reaction from the simple genuineness of early Christian belief, and how nearly the Christian world had generally associated itself, in thought and temper, not to say in superstitious practice, with the Pagan. We must not shut our eyes to the fact that much of the apparent success of the new religion had been gained by its actual accommodation of itself to the ways and feelings of the old. It was natural it should be so. Once set aside, from doubt, distaste, or any other feeling, the special dogmas of the Gospel (and the urgency of Athanasius and Augustine in establishing and giving prominence to them, shows of itself how commonly they were set aside even in the Christian communions), and men will naturally turn to compromise, to eclecticism, to universalism, to indifference, to unbelief. This was the peril of the day, which the great Christian teachers marked and combated. Among the blunders of the apostate Julian—who seems to me to have shown little sense or discretion in conducting the defence of Paganism, and to have thrown away, if ever man did, the chance which Providence, for aught we know, might have given him of suppressing for a time the name of 'the Galilean'—none was so great as that of shutting against the Christians the doors of the Pagan schools, and excluding them, as far as was possible, from participating in the fruits of the old Pagan learning. The Christians, it must be admitted, were running only too precipitately into the snare there spread for them already. They were throwing themselves, guilelessly, into the arms of Paganism, of a still living Paganism; for Pagan literature was not, could not be to them, in that era, what it has since become to us, the mere shadow of a life which has been lived out for ages. No: the schools of Athens and Alexandria, and a hundred other Pagan universities, were still open, still full of thought and life, still brooding over past recollections and presumptuous hopes; from day to day they resounded with some fresh augury of revived authority, and spiritual triumph. If the great Christian doctors had themselves come forth from the schools of the Pagans, the loss had not been wholly unrequited: so complacently had even Christian doctors again surrendered themselves to the fascinations of Pagan speculation; so fatally, in their behalf, had they extenuated Christian dogma, and acknowledged the fundamental truth and sufficiency of science falsely so called. We may respect, we may admire, perhaps, the compliments and caresses which pass between men such as Augustine and Basil, and the most distinguished teachers of these rival opinions; but how was it with Christian students of less force and firmness? Can we suppose that weaker and younger men did not suffer their courtesy to decline into compromise, their compliments to descend to acquiescence? Even Basil, whose force and firmness cannot be doubted, indulges in his correspondence with friends among the Heathen, in a laxity of language which in another could not fail to be suspicious; in one place he professes to doubt, playfully perhaps, but it was hardly a time for sport, whether the world is governed by an iron fate, or a capricious fortune, in tones which may possibly have been suggested, and seemed to justify, the well-known scepticism of the great Pagan poet of the age. Of the tone of semi-Christianity, which pervaded the literature of the age, where one dash, perhaps, of Christian truth is thrown in among pages of mere Pagan sentiment, this is not the place or opportunity to speak. But take one instance only of the apparent indifference of the Christian multitude to Christian teaching, even to its corruptions received among them, as well as to its genuine truths. The Bishop Sinesius was a famous man of letters, bred a philosopher, descended from the kings of Sparta, an admirer of the Pagan Hypatia. The people of Ptolemais demanded him for their Bishop. He protests that his life and practice are not pure enough for so holy an office; he has a wife whom he cannot abandon, as the manners of the age require; whom he will not consort with secretly, as the manners of the age, it seems, allow. 'I never will believe,' he adds, 'that the soul is born together with the body; I will never teach that the world is destined to perish; the resurrection as taught by the Church, seems to me a dubious and questionable doctrine; I cannot yield to the prejudices of the vulgar.' In short, he seems to mean: 'I am a Platonist, not a Christian.' The people leave him his wife and his opinions, and make him their Bishop. He retains his Philosophy, his Paganism, his Universalism, and continues to sit at the feet of its expounders.

Far be it from me, far be it from any of us, to repudiate or disparage the combination of a taste for letters with the cultivation of Christian sentiment. But, I repeat, there is a time for all things; and it was no time for these dallyings, when Paganism was still a power outside the Church, while dogmatic errors, closely allied to Paganism, and leading directly to it, were rampant and flourishing within it. There were, doubtless, as I have said, among the Christians of that age strong minds, on which this dangerous taste exercised no fatal influence.

There is something peculiarly touching and consoling in the kindly intercourse of the good and saintly Paulinus with the good-natured man of the world, only nominally Christian, if Christian even in name, Ausonius. The rough and vigorous Jerome remained staunchly Christian, inflexible in doctrine, to the end :—and a shrewd man of the world, too, in some respects, notwithstanding his fervent addiction to Heathen literature, his admiration, over which he himself sighs, and almost shudders, for the chiefs of profane philosophy, for his Plato and his Cicero. In his cave at Bethlehem he employed scribes to copy for him the great master works of antiquity. His own masculine spirit may have been untainted by what he himself regarded as a sweet poison ; but how it may have fared with his transcribers, he did not pause, it seems, to inquire.

This is no hollow declamation; no sour Puritanic fancy. The moment was a critical one. Paganism was not a peril to be trifled with. Another generation of the Church triumphant, of ease in the Christian Zion, and the Gospel we find was almost eaten out from the heart of the Christian society. I speak not now of the pride of its spiritual pretensions, of the corruption of its secular politics, of its ascetic extravagances, its mystical fallacies, of its hollowness in preaching, or its laxity in practice :—of its saint worship, which was a revival of hero-worship ; its addiction to the sensuous in outward service, which was a revival of idolatry. But I point to the fact less observed by our church historians, of the absolute defect of all distinctive Christianity in the utterances of men of the highest esteem as Christians, men of reputed wisdom, sentiment, and devotion. Look, for instance, at the remains we possess of the Christian Boethius; a man whom we know to have been a professed Christian and Churchman, excellent in action, steadfast in suffering, but in whose writings, in which he aspires to set before us the true grounds of spiritual consolation on which he rested himself in the hour of his trial, and on which he would have his fellows rest, there is no trace of Christianity whatever, nothing but pure unmingled naturalism. See here a conspicuous instance of the Pagan reaction of the age which succeeded Constantine: here is one example, a host in itself, of the dereliction, so to call it, from Christian dogma in a world professedly Christian. Here is a justification of the energy with which an Athanasius and an Augustine insisted on theoretic and distinctive Christianity. In spite of their teaching, unless it please you to say that it was a natural revolt against it, as excessive and tyrannical, the generation which followed them sank back into a vague, diluted, historic Christianity, which had none of the spiritual characteristics of the Gospel, none of its living force and power, none, we may apprehend, of its sanctifying and saving grace. It was, if you please, such a reaction as turned the court of Rome before the Reformation into a Pagan consistory—made popes and cardinals deride covertly the Resurrection and the Judgment, and *these fables*, as they whispered among themselves, by which we live so elegantly:—such a reaction as reduced the serious and thoughtful Church of England of the seventeenth century to the pale morality and cold materialism of the eighteenth;—such, let me add, as in still later times has replaced the austere dogmatism of a few years back by the fitful and fretful indifferentism which holds out its languid hands to infidelity and superstition among ourselves.[1]

But see in conclusion how this decline of distinctive Christian belief was accompanied with a marked decline of Christian morality. Heathenism reasserted its empire over the carnal affections of the natural man. The pictures of abounding wickedness in the high places and the low places of the earth, which are presented to us by the witnesses of the worst Pagan degradation, are repeated, in colours not less strong, in lines not less hideous, by the observers of the gross and reckless iniquity of the so-called Christian period now before us. It becomes evident that as the great mass of the careless and indifferent have assumed with the establishment of the Christian Church in authority and honour, the outward garb and profession of Christian believers, so with the decline of belief, the corruption of the visible Church, the same masses, indifferent and irreligious as of old, have rejected the moral restraints which their profession should have imposed upon them.

Let us fix our eyes for a few moments upon these symptoms, their causes and their consequences.

[1] Notes and Illustrations (E).

The Pagans had run through their intellectual and spiritual course: like the aged emperor on his death-bed, the once vigorous and restless conqueror, now subdued by pain and weakness, and reduced to contemplate, from his low estate, the vanity of his efforts and his triumphs, they might exclaim with Severus, 'I have been everything, and nothing has answered.' They had tried every speculation of the human mind so as to seize, if it might be, the truths of morals and religion, and so find rest for their souls; and nothing had succeeded with them. The fantastic visions of philosophy had replaced the trivialities of mythology; and these again had been discarded for the monstrosities of magic and mysticism. But nought had served to quiet their conscience, to calm their terrors, and assuage their remorse, to bring them nearer to God. At last they had thrown themselves, with a divine impulse, upon Christ, and had found in Him a faith and a hope.

But we must not imagine that man, thus turned to God in the decrepitude of age, or in the weakness of his last sickness, can serve Him, even for the brief remnant of his days, with a lusty and effectual service. In the Christian faith of the converted empire we must not look for the vigour, the simplicity, and the self-devotion which are required for carrying on God's work, for showing forth its strength and beauty, for propagating vigorous offshoots throughout the world. The development of the Church after Constantine partook of the sickness and infirmity of that enervated society in which it was cast. We marvel sometimes, we feel disappointment, or even dismay, at the apparent failure of the pure and holy Gospel, when full play, full power, full authority, were first given to it among men. Granting all the greatness of the greatest men of the Church triumphant—of its Augustine, its Chrysostom, its Jerome, its Ambrosius—how much greater than any of the contemporary heathen!—granting the fresh spiritual tone it infused into legislation; the higher tone of its polity; its clearer appreciation of duty; its nearer sense of the divine; the loftier rule it preached, at least, of holiness and goodness:—granted that the Holy Spirit really brooded over it, and showed forth His presence by signs, such as have never been wholly wanting to it in any stage of its progress;—nevertheless, men remarked with pain and perplexity how far Christianity—established, favoured, and protected—fell short of the promise it had given in weakness, in obscurity, or in persecution; how far it had fallen from the bright ideal inscribed in letters of light on the pages of its heavenly credentials.

But men judge the Gospel wrongly. They do not regard, as they should do, the materials on which it had now to exert itself; the mass of decay, decrepitude, corruption, which it was summoned to enliven and regenerate. The conversion of the Empire was the effort of the old age of civilization to throw off the humours which were devouring its very life; to revive its lost strength; to straighten the bent limbs; to smooth the wrinkles on its countenance; to renew its youth as the wings of the young eagle. It had run to many quacks and pretenders, and all that human science could do had been done for it. At last, it had resorted to the true Physician of Souls; it had drunk of the waters of spiritual life, but they were no elixir of physical renovation. The decay of the vital powers of Roman society was beyond cure. Jesus Christ had no medicine for the sickness of the body politic. All our admiration for the great names of the Church of Nicæa cannot blind us to her imperfect apprehension of divine truth, and the still more imperfect practice of her children. We know how grievously she erred in suppressing many truths, in exalting to undue eminence some graces doubtful at the best, and easily swoln or perverted into errors. 'How is the gold become dim! how is the most fine gold changed!'[1] It was in the epoch of her greatest power and grandeur that Jerome, moved with holy fervour, threatened to write her history, as the most terrible of protests against her, of which the theme and burden should be the four scathing words, 'Greater in riches, less in virtues.'

This is not, be assured, the idle retrospect of later ages, exulting, vainly perhaps, in superior knowledge or sanctity of its own. It is not the judgment of a Reformed Church looking askance at the faults and weaknesses of an age which laid, no doubt, the foundation of many of the grossest corruptions of later times. No: it is the grave and repeated assertion of the best and wisest contemporaries.

[1] Lamentations iv. 1.

From the age of Cyprian downwards, when the first symptoms of moral degeneracy were noticed, the chain of witnesses to this decline is close and unbroken. We read it in the rude satire of Commodian, in the earnest pathos of Augustine, in the politic wisdom of Ambrose. We read it again in the indignant rhetoric of Salvian, in the courtlier survey of the gentle Sidonius. The Acts of Severinus, the apostle of Bavaria, attest it; the laments of our British historian, the so-called Gildas, derive from it their greatest poignancy. And there is no witness to it more grave, perhaps, and trustworthy, than the great Roman bishop Leo; none whose declarations on the subject may be deemed more striking and conclusive.

The utter laxity of moral conduct which had thus succeeded to the strictness of living in the early Christian society is, by these men and others, too closely investigated and exposed; it is too plainly and numerously attested to admit of doubt or extenuation. It runs back into the old Pagan channels with a precision too natural for fiction. The temples, the sacrifices, the public shows and festivals, reassert their hold on the imagination: the vices to which Paganism had lent her cloak or sanction claim again connivance, indulgence, and authorization. The preacher calls aloud for a special intervention of God to sustain the weak and weary efforts of His Church now vainly militant upon earth. 'So does iniquity abound' (such is the common tone of his complaints), 'that either all men are themselves bad, or, if good, they are cruelly persecuted by the many:' 'thus are verified the words of the apostle, "The whole world lieth in wickedness."' 'No wonder worse and worse daily befalls us, who are becoming more wicked daily.'

But 'that which decayeth and waxeth old is ready to vanish away.'[1] The foe was now nigh at hand, even at the door. From day to day, from year to year, came on the invading barbarian, sapping and mining with stubborn perseverance the bulwarks of the Roman empire. Then mourned the Church in sackcloth and in ashes; and above the din of arms and the murmurs of lamentation was heard the voice of the priest and preacher, explaining and vindicating the chastisements of Providence, which, long provoked and forbearing, now laid all the weight of its arm upon her. Her sins had long called out for vengeance; and behold! vengeance had overtaken her. Strickened and dismayed, she still turned not heartily to God. She was too far gone in her wickedness to repent. Her last state was worse than her first; for the sense of the divine retribution had soured and hardened her; her levity had turned to stubbornness, her disobedience to blasphemy and unbelief. In the east and west, the north and the south, according to the concurring testimony of affrighted observers, the same phenomena were distinctly visible; the signs of a general degeneracy, of an impending relapse into Paganism, even in new and monstrous forms,

[1] Heb. viii. 13.

befitting the senile decrepitude of a world on its death-bed. It was an augury of judgment no longer to be delayed; for '[1] that which beareth thorns and briars is rejected, and is nigh unto cursing: whose end is to be burned.'[2]

[1] Heb. vi. 8.

[2] Notes and Illustrations (F).

LECTURE V.

PREPARATION OF THE NORTHERN NATIONS FOR THE RECEPTION OF CHRISTIANITY.

St. Luke i. 80.

And the child grew and waxed strong in spirit, and was in the deserts till the day of his shewing unto Israel.

The contrast between youth and age so vividly presented to us in the opening chapter of St. Luke's Gospel has a solemn interest for all men. The contrast in the mere outward lineaments, as it appeared to the bystanders, between John and his aged parents, between the infant Jesus and Joseph and Simeon, is heightened to the eye of faith by our sense of the deeper moral contrast involved in it; and from this spiritual intuition the great painters of sacred story have drawn no small portion of their energy in imagining and portraying. I too would invite you to consider it in its spiritual bearing, and see in it the operation of God's providence in the religious training of His creatures.

First stands before us an ancient priest named Zacharias, with his aged wife Elizabeth, both descended from the priestly race, both righteous before God, walking in all the commandments and ordinances of the law blameless; both doubtless feeling deeply the corruption of their age, the sinfulness of their people, and the drawing back of God's hand from the children of His promise, the veiling of His face before their abounding iniquity. They had no child, and both were now well-stricken in years; they could not hope to leave behind them a root of righteousness sprung from their own holy stock; they could bequeath no seed of renovation to a world far sunk in sinfulness and corruption. Then God Himself intervenes. An angel conveys His message of grace and hope. What man could not anticipate, and natural order could not produce, shall be effected by a special Providence from on high. 'Fear not, Zacharias; thy prayer is heard, . . . thy wife shall bear thee a son. . . . Thou shalt have joy and gladness, and many shall rejoice at his birth. . . . Many of the children of Israel shall he turn to the Lord their God: and he shall go before Him in the spirit and power of Elias, . . . to make ready a people prepared for the Lord.' [1]

And then pass on to the period of the months completed, and behold this promised child, this destined messenger, this appointed instrument of grace to men, brought forth among his assembled kindred for enrolment in the Church of the Covenant:—mark the fulfilment of the token by which the promise should be attested, and the glorious confidence with which, on its fulfilment, the favoured father bursts into prophetic num-

[1] St. Luke i. 13–17.

bers. His mouth was opened, and his tongue was loosed, and he spake and praised God. He was filled with the Holy Ghost, and prophesied, saying, 'Blessed be the Lord God of Israel, for He hath visited and redeemed His people; And hath raised up a horn of salvation for us in the house of His servant David. And thou, Child, shalt be called the Prophet of the Highest; for thou shalt go before the face of the Lord to prepare His ways, to give knowledge of salvation unto His people by the remission of their sins, through the tender mercy of our God; whereby the day-spring from on high hath visited us.'

Thus at the very outset of the Gospel our attention is arrested, our imagination is roused, by the contrast so vividly brought before us between the aged believer, just about to quit the scene of his faithful labours, in hope and peace, and the infant child on whom his hope and faith repose, whose career is all before him—a career of faithful labour and of spiritual endurance. A world is rolling away, a new world is gliding in. We feel our sympathy attracted, according to the temper of each of us, to the old man about to depart, or to the infant of whom so great a future is promised: to the past achievments of faith and obedience, or to the future auguries of hope. We look to the gray hairs and the staff which supports the tottering steps, and again to the child in its mother's arms, to the cradle in which it has been resting. The imagination seems instinctively to realize on the one hand the genius of the past, on the other the genius of the future. In Zacharias we remark the minister of a religion appointed for a time; in John the herald of a kingdom to endure for everlasting.

The scene of Zacharias returning thanks for the birth of John is a prelude to another and a still more solemn one which is soon to follow, when the aged Simeon blesses God for the greater revelation of the infant Jesus: 'Lord, now lettest Thou Thy servant depart in peace, according to Thy word, for mine eyes have seen Thy salvation, which Thou hast prepared before the face of all people; a light to lighten the Gentiles, and to be the glory of Thy people Israel.'

Such contrasts between youth and age, between the past and the future, occur elsewhere in Scripture; and trained as we are by our Christian faith to look ever forward for new manifestations of divine grace and power, they tend to preserve in us a fresh and living sense of the progress of the divine dispensations. God, we feel, is the same God from generation to generation; ever creating afresh from the old materials; ever producing life out of death, vigour out of decay; ever casting off the old plumes and feathers, and renewing mankind like the young eagles.

But these contrasts are not always thus joyous and serene. It is not always a contrast between the good and faithful servant who has done his work, and is about to enter into the joy of his Lord, and the youthful disciple who is to succeed him and surpass him. We have a more painful contrast, yet one not less significant and instructive, in the relations between Eli and Samuel presented to us in the Old Testament.

Here too the child, like John, like Jesus, is highly favoured of God. He too grows up in favour with God and man. He is set up for the instruction of his people, to be the strength and glory of Israel, to the glory of God, to the manifestation of his own faith and obedience. His work is less highly exalted than that of the Baptist, the herald of the spiritual Day-spring; his sphere is more limited, his means less powerful, his influence less conspicuous. Nevertheless he has his stated part to play in the divine economy. For this he is prepared by a special dispensation. To this he is devoted from his birth, kept apart from men, and consecrated to the Lord. He too is a pattern child, and grows to be a pattern man; to bear the full weight of God's command upon his shoulder and to bear them triumphantly to the end. But not so Eli. The aged Judge of Israel is not to be compared for faith and sanctity with the righteous Zacharias or the devout Simeon. He is rather set before us as a warning. He bears indeed a part in the economy of God's dispensation. He is an instrument in God's hands, and not a mere worthless instrument. He is not wholly reprobate. He rules his people perhaps with some sense of justice; he teaches them with some sense of truth; he is not insensible to the beauty of holiness, or indifferent to the blessings of grace. He feels the motions of natural affection; but his natural affection, unchecked and unchastened by a higher law, becomes his snare, and effects his downfall. His virtues are mellowed and corrupted into sins, and have become to him an occasion of falling. And these sins have grown upon him and entwined themselves around him, till they smother the seeds of grace in his heart; and he will not tear them off and trample them down. Therefore through the wickedness of the children whom he has indulged, and set up in God's place in his heart, he brings Israel to ruin, his family to shame, himself to despair and death.

How often and how strikingly is this contrast presented to the view of the Christian minister in the course of his ordinary duties!

He visits the death-bed of the aged—how various, how opposed in its experiences bodily and mental!—the scene sometimes of tranquil decline and painless dissolution, with the sweet consolations of faith and hope, with the comfortable recollection of past mercies, resignation to the will of Him who has been found ever kind and gracious; sometimes of more fervid joy and triumphant expectations; how often again disturbed by bodily suffering in all its forms; by mental agitation not less manifold; by contrition and remorse; by apprehension and despair; sometimes by indignation and defiance; by pride and vainglorious confidence; sometimes by womanly regrets; sometimes by mere disgust and weariness. He probes the soul of the dull or hardened; he terrifies the obdurate; he binds up the broken-hearted. He winds his way through the snares and artifices with which the craft of intellect has been wont to fetter or benumb the conscience. He holds up the lamp of truth to eyes which have been long shut against light and knowledge; or have mistaken the false shows of this world for the genuine reflection of the brightness of God's person.

But leaving the bedside of the dying, he betakes himself next moment to the seat of the teacher in the school. Here stands before him the rude material of which Cnrist's Church of the future is to be formed, in its simplicity and innocence, its fervour and impetuosity, its zeal and courage, untried by temptation, untempered by suffering, unknown to itself, its destiny hidden in the bosom of a watchful Providence; a new generation, which shall be set for the rising and the falling of many in Christendom; of whom we can only say, in the profound darkness of the future, that assuredly it has a marked and definite part to play in the course of man's spiritual history, whether for good or for evil; that it is already an instrument in God's hand for the furtherance of his deep designs, to speed onwards in its appointed path the course of His adorable dispensations.

The minister stands for the moment between the two generations, at the middle point of the present; and full of faith and confidence in the fulfilment of the divine promises, believes and trusts that both work together to a common end; and marvels at the power of the Almighty, which on the one hand makes itself witnesses in the seared heart and manifold experiences of age, on the other establishes His truth by the mouths of babes and sucklings.

In the aged Zacharias and the child John we have beheld the contrast between two dispensations; the one fading away and about to perish, the other coming forth into the world in new life and freshness. But of the early career of this representative child very little is recorded; nor more of his training for his holy mission; but that his mother dedicated him from his birth to the service of God, according to the usages of her countrymen, and that presently, as the text says, 'the child grew and waxed strong in spirit, and was in the deserts'—was removed from the ordinary abodes and habits of men to a rude solitude—and there continued under God's teaching for about thirty years, 'till the day of his shewing unto Israel.' We are led to infer that the solitude of a hermit in the wilderness—separated from the world, seclusion from its glare and noise, unacquaintance with its vicious ways and fashions, with its common training and the prejudices thence derived—was necessary for receiving the fulness of divine inspiration; that a vessel of so much grace must be kept from the first holy and undefiled; that one who was set to teach God's word with peculiar energy and power must receive it direct from Him; not manipulated by human hands, not interpreted by human glosses, not filtered through human channels.

And so it was also with one who was greater than John the Baptist, with one who was not the least, but among the first in the kingdom of heaven; so it was with Saul the convert of Jesus Christ; who when it pleased God to 'reveal His Son' in him, that he 'might preach Him among the Heathen,' immediately 'conferred not with flesh and blood;'[1] neither did he 'go up to Jerusalem to them which were apostles' before him; but he went into Arabia; and from thence to Damascus, and Syria, and Cilicia, avoiding the conversation of the brethren in the churches, so as to be unknown by face to the disciples in Judea:—doubtless that none might have the first teaching and training of this vessel of grace but God Himself through the operation of the Holy Spirit.

And so—to apply the parallel to the argument before us—so when God was about to cast away, as if disappointed and repenting of His work, the instruments of His grace whom, next after the Jews, He had chosen for the building of His Church and the diffusion of His truth; when He was about to humble and cast down the Greek and Roman Churches which had been called out from among the heathen of the Empire, and which had grown and prospered under His hand till they comprehended the Empire itself; He prepared long in secret and in solitude the people, the human instruments of His policy, the human vessels of His grace, by whom He purposed to replace them.

The Greeks and Romans, the bright and polished children of the South, had failed to fulfil the task im-

[1] Galat. i. 16.

posed upon them. They had broken down through the infirmity of corruptions. Faith, accedted slowly, embraced coldly, had produced no fruit of holiness and purity, and languished in the sphere of their effete society. A new material was to be called forth; a new mass of ore to be stamped with the image of Christ's revelation; the nations of the North—Goths and Franks, Burgundians and Saxons—were to be thrust into the place of which *they* had shown themselves unworthy; were to sit upon *their* thrones, to inherit *their* patrimony, to succeed to *their* spiritual privileges. And these nations must have their long and patient training for the task so graciously imposed upon them; these children of the new era must be separated and kept apart in holy dedication to their divine calling, howbeit themselves unconscious of their mission. They, too, like the child John, shall wax great and strong in spirit, and continue in the deserts until the day of their showing unto Christendom.

From these nations of the North we are for the most part ourselves descended. Their blood flows in our veins: their character is impressed upon our minds: our language speaks to us of them; our laws represent to us their notions of right and justice; our worship is founded on the conceptions they embraced of deity and spirit, of the divine calling of men and of women. Through many an age these ideas have been working in them and their descendants, gathering around us fold upon fold of inward and outward knowledge; utilizing spiritual experiences; applying foreign materials; assimilating the best elements of religious consciousness from all sides; fructifying in the bosom of time, and bringing forth in their season new and vigorous offshoots of the truth once implanted in them. Through these Northern peoples, these barbarians, as they have so often been called, we have derived our Christianity: for they took to themselves and applied to their own spiritual necessities the truth they found dishonoured or forgotten in the Empire, clasping it with fervour to their hearts, and making it their own by right of derelict; moulding it, perchance, with the pressure of their own right hand; colouring it, it may be, with the hues of their own spiritual imagination.

About the primitive history of human progress there are two conflicting opinions: the solution of the question awaits, perhaps, another generation. Let us not be too hasty to dogmatize about it. The ancients generally believed in an original creation of man in a state approaching to moral perfection; a state from which he declined by regular steps, from a golden age to a silver, a brazen, and an iron:—a pleasing and fanciful illustration of a deep thought, of the regrets and remorse of a self-accusing conscience. But this sense of guilt, this tone of self-accusation, however suited to the simple unsophisticated feelings of mankind, was unpalatable to the pride of the philosophers. The schools of Greece and Rome discarded the tradition of the ancients, as beneath the dignity of man, and assumed as the discovery of moral self-inquiry, that man on the contrary was first created, or first sprang, perchance, spontaneously, in form and faculties most rude and degraded, and, after ages of grovelling barbarism, worked his own way upwards, by his own efforts, or with the aid, it may be, of a kindly fortune, from a state akin to the lower animals to the full nobility of kings and sages.

It has been held, however, for three thousand years at least, by that portion of mankind which has resorted to the Jewish Scriptures for the first and truest records of primitive history, that the former of these opinions comes nearest to the fact: that man has from the first been placed on earth with a full capacity for the highest civilization, for the noblest ideas, the truest intellectual and moral culture: that his spiritual conceptions, more especially, have alighted upon him from an original inspiration, a teaching imparted to him at his birth, or together with his first social development.

Again, the philosophers of modern times, true to their natural filiation from the sceptics of Greece and Rome, seek to divest us of all the reverence we entertain for the spiritual teaching of our forefathers, by assuring us that we, the men of this age and generation, are really the crown of human growth and progress: that all that went before us were much inferior to us; squalid and savage men—monkeys, it may be, or molluscs: that God created man—if He did indeed create him—little if at all better than the brutes; and that all our advance, from first to last, is due to chance or fate, or the irreversible law of progress, by the natural disappearance of the lowest and survival of the highest organizations. And they can go, no doubt, a step beyond their predecessors in such-like speculations; for they make their appeal to physical phenomena—scanty and meagre, I may be allowed to say, as yet, for the support of so tremendous a theory;—a theory, however, of which it behoves us to speak with respect, as legitimate in point of method, however little the apprehension we need feel regarding it.

The appeal is to physical science; and the answer must come from those who are skilled in the mysteries of the material world. Such an answer may not be the only one, nor the most sure and satisfactory; but at all events it may be fairly demanded of those who are capable of rendering it. For my own part, I cannot pretend to meet the philosophers on this ground; nor can I say how far the records of religion depend for their acceptance on the results of inquiry into mere physical phenomena. These are questions which will be argued to the full in the years that are before us; and God, I believe, who has not failed His Church, or His humble seekers, for so many ages, will not suffer their faith to fail for lack of adequate support in this or any other trial in store for it.

But I venture meanwhile to ask these speculators to produce any instance of spiritual progress among the races of mankind, which can support their theory of gradual advance from the state of the brute or barbarian to that of Saint or Sage either of Paganism or Christianity. Do we know of any nation or kindred — Greek or German or Indian — of which it can be asserted, — There was once a time when this people were as low in the scale of humanity as are now the bushmen of Papua or New Holland; but see how, step by step, from school to school, from intuition to intuition, they evolved a Homer or a Menu, a Paul or a Luther? Were the Greeks, the Germans, the Indians, for instance, as far back as we can trace them, ever destitute of a spiritual culture, the same in kind at least, not of course in degree, as at the highest culmination of their history? Is not the evidence as strong,—nay stronger,—that the savages now existing around us are the degenerate offshoots of civilized races, as that the civilized are the cream and efflorescence of the savage?

Look more particularly at the people of whom I am now to speak, at the German nations, as a type of the Northern races generally; look at the earliest records we possess of them, in their state of rude material deficiency, which we call their barbarism; when they roamed their annual course from pasture to pasture; when they had no cities, no roads, or other appliances of what we denominate civilization; when they had not yet polished their native tongue into an instrument of recorded sentiment: — still, even in the few pages consecrated to their memory by the supercilious Romans, we may trace already among them the greatest results of true moral culture. They have already acquired a deep reverential sense of spiritual things; a profound respect for the voice of God speaking with authority through human organs; a sense of divine government and providence; a conscience active and inquisitive; suspicion at least of sinfulness; apprehension of punishment; longing for forgiveness; a passion for sacrifice and atonement. They are noted by the materialists who observe them for their spiritual conception of Deity as a Being not to be represented by sensuous images, not to be confined within the precincts of a material building; a dweller in the heavens above, or in the earth beneath, who approaches nighest to his worshippers in the wide prospect from the mountain top, or in the deep seclusion of the forest. They have attained a respect for human life, and a sense of responsibility in regard to it, such as shames the morbid hardheartedness of a fastidious civilization. They have secured one of the best and strongest incentives to virtuous exertion, one of the surest pledges of spiritual progress, in their fine appreciation of the worth of the female character. Man and woman, in their view, are sanctified by direct connection with the divine, and by the promise of eternal re-union with it. They believe in an immortality hereafter, the foundation of all virtue and courage here.[1]

And further, speaking of the Gothic nations broadly, we may trace in the particulars of their belief an ap-

[1] Notes and Illustrations (G).

proach to much which we trust we have learned from the source of truth more directly ourselves. Such are the formation of the world out of chaos; the creation of man; his primitive state of innocence and happiness; the fall of his godlike nature, which they ascribed to his mingling with the accursed Giants; the existence of a Spirit of Evil; and of a Tree of Life.

The Spirit of Evil has assumed to them a form and substance in the person of the Giants who have risen against God. Odin is the champion of God against them. Released from the physical ideas of elemental disturbance which lay perhaps at its foundation, this struggle acquired in their minds a moral significance. It was transferred from Odin, the crown and flower of man, to man himself, and man was supposed to be engaged in an eternal conflict with the spirit, not of physical, but of moral evil, of sin and selfishness. Conflict became, in the view of the Northern people, the appointed condition of man's existence. The lusts of soul and body were marked as his eternal enemies. Hence their whole career in life acquired a warlike character. Life was to them a parable illustrating the natural antagonism of sin and spirit. Odin, the Spirit which penetrates and enlivens all things, becomes preëminently the War-God, and challenges the highest place in the imagination of his worshippers. His inspiration is courage and martial ardour. The brave who fall in battle revive under his dispensation; he receives them from his attendant spirits, and places them in the paradise of the North.

In this doctrine, viewed in its material and carnal aspects, there was an anticipation of the teaching of the Jewish Scriptures, which proclaimed as with the voice of the trumpet and clarion, 'The Lord is a man of war.' 'The Lord shall go forth as a mighty man; he shall stir up jealousy like a man of war.'[1] But taken spiritually, as it would be handled and moulded by Christian missionaries, it might prepare the mind of the believer for the Christian revelation of the soul's warfare with evil. It might speak in tones according with the martial imagery of the Gospel: for the Gospel too abounds in figures of war and combat, and speaks of the sword of faith, and the helmet of salvation, and the fiery darts of the wicked one, and the whole armour of God.

But the special doctrine of the Christian Scriptures is approached at least in the Northern mythology. The Revelation of Jesus Christ as the Great Sacrifice casts its shadow before it in the traditions of the Edda. Balder, as we there read, the son of Odin, is the fairest and best of beings; beloved of gods and men. He bears indeed the national character of the warrior; he is the giver of strength in combat; he goes forth conquering and to conquer. But no less is he the perfect expression of innocence, holiness, and justice. His judgments stand for ever: none can gainsay them. He gathers in him-

[1] Exod. xv. 3. Isaiah xlii. 13.

self all the attributes of the Deity, various, and to human views conflicting,—yet such as God has Himself revealed them to us,—of justice and mercy, of love and anger, of force and persuasion. But this being, excellent and godlike, falls at last by the craft and malice of the Devil. All nature weeps; gods and men weep; all weep but the Devil only; and for the want of the tears of the Evil One he cannot return to bless men on earth with his presence any more. The crowning idea of redemption through the God-man's sufferings is thus crippled and curtailed: it is postponed to the future, relegated to some final dispensation; when the Evil Power Loki, and Death, the wolf-god Fenris, shall be bound in Hell for ever, and the powers of Heaven shall triumph in the glorious consummation of all things.[1]

Such are some of the points of analogy between the traditions of the Edda and the Christian Scriptures: such the anticipations which might seem to await completion in the revelation of Jesus Christ; such the distant guidance of the Holy Spirit of God vouchsafed to the nations of the North. And they were not unworthy for whom such special ministrations should be appointed. They were prepared to accept and profit by them by their natural docility and moral tendencies, by their aptness to assimilate the lessons of material and spiritual culture.

But it would lead me far away from the train of thought and the language suitable to this place and oc-

[1] Notes and Illustrations (H).

casion, were I to trace, however briefly, the tokens to which I have only pointed, of this peculiar characteristic of the Northern nations. For four centuries they stood face to face with the great conquerors and civilizers of the South, watchful but not subservient; emulous but still jealously independent. Their greatest warriors had been trained in the camps of their Roman rivals. In the arts of peace the German was a skilful imitator. He built his towns, he cultivated his fields, he surrounded himself with the appliances of luxury, after the pattern learned from the masters of human civilization. Even the religious ideas of those before him he quickly assimilated; he adapted their traditions to his own; imbibed their thoughts; sympathized with their aspirations. When the time arrived for the fusion of the two races, the traveller standing on the banks of their frontier rivers, might ask himself, viewing the monuments of civil life on either hand around him, which side was the Roman and which the German.

If then we admire in any work of man's hand the evidence of a cunning design, the tokens of a thoughtful foresight; if we worship reverently the hand of the Divine artificer in the adaptation of means to ends in the outward frame of nature: in the limbs of animals; in the foliage of trees; in the processes of life and death; in the structure of the universe;—not less should we remark and admire divine contrivance in the moulding of a national character for the great religious purpose to which it is destined to be applied. For ages this purpose has seemed to slumber in the breast of the All-disposer; for ages the races of the North—the barbarians as we call them, as the Romans called them slightingly—roamed their deserts unnoticed by the trained and civilized among men. For ages no sage or seer of Greece or Rome, of Egypt or Palestine, had dreamed of the power latent in those savage regions, of the dispensation slumbering in those untutored bosoms; for the time had not yet arrived for putting them to their proper use. The Greek and Roman were still on their trial; the Jew was still on his trial, unto whom were still committed the oracles of God. But God Himself was still silently watching over them; and so they grew and waxed strong in spirit, and were in the deserts till the day of their showing to the Empire.

That day, speaking broadly, came with great suddenness, and that manifestation might seem at once complete. The conquest of the Empire and the conversion of the Northern races, might be regarded, in a general view, as one great historical event. Looking more closely, indeed, we see that, like all wide-reaching revolutions, these issues were in fact slow and gradual, the providential development of many causes and myriads of interwoven incidents. The intercourse of the rival races for four centuries along two thousand miles of frontier had been varied, and their action upon one another reciprocal. The Empire, for instance, had received the importation of many thousands of captives from the North, and to the poor captive, the desolate stranger, the tormented slave, the Gospel and the Church, embosomed in the Empire, had spoken with force and conviction. To him Jesus Christ had been father and mother, and wife and lands. The North again had invited an immigration of crowds of persecuted believers, fugitives from the chain and the axe, and the lions of the amphitheatre. Jesus Christ had guided their steps and lightened the burden of their pilgrimage. Rome, once more, had surrounded herself with legions of foreign auxiliaries, recruited from the Scythians and the Germans; and among them holy men had laboured, and converted them into an army of Christ. And from these in turn had gone forth missionaries of the Faith, such as Ulfilas, the wolf-born, become the apostle of the barbarians, the translator of the Scriptures into the Gothic tongue;—the Moses, as he was boldly designated, of the Goths—who had descended from the mystic presence in the holy place, from the metropolitan temple of the Holy Wisdom of God, bearing the written tidings of salvation to his admiring and expecting countrymen.[1]

Thus the nations of the North were gradually prepared for their complete and final conversion. The Lord had been 'preached to them that were afar off;' 'the inhabitants of the isles had been astonished at Him.'[2] 'There was no speech or language' where the voice of the preacher had not been heard; 'his line was gone forth throughout the earth, and his words to the end of the world.'[3] The Church of the Empire, in its

[1] Notes and Illustrations (I). [2] Ezek. xxvii. 35. [3] Ps. xix. 4.

own alarms and anxieties, was looking for the result; and the sanguine soul of Jerome, from his retreat in Bethlehem, cast a raptured glance on the triumphant progress of the Spirit, and the glorious tokens of the future about to be revealed. 'Who would believe it'— he exclaims: 'that the barbarous Gothic tongue should seek the truth of the Hebrew; that while the Greek is slumbering or wrangling, the German should explore the sayings of the Holy Spirit? Of a truth I know that God is no respecter of persons; but that in every nation he that feareth God and worketh righteousness is accepted of Him. Lo! the hands once hardened by the sword-hilt, fingers once fitted to the bowstring, have turned to the stylus and the pen; the fierce heart of the warrior is softened to Christian mildness; and now we see fulfilled the prophecy of Isaiah, "They shall beat their swords into ploughshares, and their spears into pruning hooks: nation shall not lift up sword against nation, neither shall they learn war any more."'[1]

And again, with the same exulting confidence, 'Lo! the Armenian lays down his quiver; the Huns are learning the Psalter; the frosts of Scythia glow with the warmth of faith; the ruddy armies of the Goths bear about with them the tabernacles of the Church; and therefore, perhaps, do they fight with equal fortune against us, because equally with us they trust in the religion of Christ.'[2]

Such were the vows and aspirations of the Christians,

[1] Isaiah ii. 4. [2] Notes and Illustrations (J).

while the North was blackening with all its clouds: one-half of them did the Spirit of God accept and ratify, the other He dispersed in empty air. But of these various issues—the despair, the agony, and the triumph—I shall speak to you at another meeting.

LECTURE VI.

CONVERSION OF THE NORTHERN NATIONS.

MATT. VII. 29.

For He taught them as one having authority.

THE authority which marked our blessed Lord's teaching was purely moral and spiritual. Appearing as a mere man among men He assumed, we may believe, no personal recommendations, no comeliness or majesty, or force of eloquence or commanding power, to strike deep and sudden impression upon His hearers. From time to time, indeed, He put forth signs and wonders, performing miraculous cures and other marvellous works by hand or by word only; but we are not bid remark the appearance of authority which these actions bore: their power spoke for itself. But it was when He taught, and moreover when He taught in His mildest and most loving tones—when He gave His lessons of mercy and charity in the Sermon on the Mount—when He divested Himself most completely of all ensigns of command and Divine power—that His figure, His tones, His gestures, the circumstances amid which He spoke and the character of His teaching, conveyed most impressively to His hearers the tokens of authority. Sitting on the green hill-side, ministered unto by twelve humble companions, surrounded by a multitude of curious and attentive listeners—of men who had left the courts of the city, the imperious ordinances of the Scribes and the Pharisees, the carnal regulations of the Temple, and the commands of rulers temporal and spiritual—He delivered simple lessons of love and holiness, with a force of reasoning, an assurance of truth, which seemed at once to seal them with the sanction of God Himself.

The speaker has ceased to speak; the words remain. The teacher has returned to heaven, from whence He came; the lesson survives, inscribed in the pages of the volume which He has bequeathed to mankind as His precious legacy, stored up in the living traditions of a church which He has founded to execute and administrate His will—deeply graven in the hearts of the disciples whom from age to age have successively learned, and never failed to register and transmit them. Whatever be the truest and surest means He has provided for the safe keeping of His lessons of Truth—whether the Book or the Church or the conscience of man—the lessons themselves have been safely treasured up from that time to the present, and will remain, we doubt not, to the end of the world. Men will still continue, from age to age, to picture to themselves the scene once enacted on the Mount, when the Man Jesus addressed His disciples, and opened His mouth, and taught them those simple lessons of love and goodness which at once struck the hearts and claimed the veneration of the multitude around them.

Never again has the Lord Jesus appeared to men as He appeared in that holy place in the period of His earthly sojourn. The Sermon on the Mount was a type of His personal teaching, such as can never be repeated in His personal absence from the world. Never again can the same teaching be conveyed with the same sanctity, the same simplicity, or impress men with the same sense of Divine power and authority. Nevertheless, from age to age the lesson has been repeated, under every variety of attending circumstances, with every degree of force and persuasiveness; and blessed are they who, looking beyond the outward form of their preacher, whoever he may be, still see from age to age the holiness of the lesson—still recognise its binding force, its transcendent authority over the conscience. From day to day Jesus Christ makes experiment of His power on the individual conscience; and some men He brings under the control of His teaching, some He casts away, after trial, as unworthy and irreclaimable. If His teaching fail in any one case, it is surely from no lack of power in the doctrine, but of power in the instrument by whom He suffers it to be delivered. The instrument may often be unworthy—a vessel not of grace but of wrath; and the issue of its teaching may accord therewith. It may happen that throughout whole churches and societies, and for ages together, the teaching of Jesus may thus be imperfectly or impurely conveyed, the authority it bears may thus be sullied or maimed; it may sink in force and efficiency even below the teaching of the Scribes and the Pharisees; it may sound as hollow as the sermons in the Temple and the Synagogue. But the Divine Preacher is meanwhile watching over it, and guiding it from master to master, from revival to revival, to the unseen conclusions laid up for it in the bosom of the Eternal. Jesus Christ is still, as ever, about His Father's business. He works with the materials before Him—with the human souls which the Father has put under His teaching—with the circumstances in which they are placed, the peculiar trials and hindrances by which they are surrounded. The authority with which He teaches them is manifold and diverse, making itself all things to all men that it may gain some.

Look, for instance, at the Church of Christ as she stood in the face of the invading barbarians. We have seen that she was corrupt in practice and in doctrine—that she encouraged usages repugnant to her Lord's simple character—required obedience unreasoning and servile—cherished within her bosom the germs of a carelessness and unbelief which threatened quickly to reduce her once more under the influences of spiritual Paganism. Assuredly the Church did not meet the Northern Nations with the same pure and holy spirit with which she had confronted the Greeks and the Romans. God's arm was indeed outstretched for her protection, and His Spirit was still brooding over her, and maintaining the foundation of truth within her; but the outward testimony of miracles and of inspiration had been long withdrawn; the powers she wielded were for the most part the powers of the earth; the authority with which she might seem to speak was derived directly from her temporal condition; the spirit she communicated to her children was distilled from the fountain of Divine teaching through many impure, many imperfect channels. The task before her was more arduous, the crisis of the faith might seem more perilous, than ever before; and how much weaker her faith, her spiritual means how crippled and enfeebled!

It was indeed a period when the voice of one claiming to speak with authority was especially required. The barbarians were too fierce to be moved by the accents of charity—too sanguine and confident to regard the appeals of a reproachful conscience. They felt no sting of sinfulness—they acknowledged no call to repentance and newness of life. The moral sense lay as yet unstirred within them. Their minds, least of all, were trained to appreciate argument. Like children, they could be arrested and guided only by the tone of authority; and, like children, to the tones of authority they were disposed instinctively to hearken.

We might suppose, perhaps, that the natural impulse of warlike barbarians, emerging from their native forests, and entering on the inheritance of an effete civilization which had crumbled at their touch, would be to sweep it all scornfully away, to reject every lesson of its teaching, to extinguish the flicker of its spiritual life, and establish in its place the fancies and traditions of their own untrained imagination.

Such might be our expectations; but the result was just the contrary. Arrived within the frontiers of the Empire, the strangers became deeply impressed with the majesty of the features it presented to them. They had been moulded and prepared in secret by Providence for the part now thrust upon them. They were not brought suddenly and unexpectedly face to face with the religion of the world they had conquered. Christianity, as we have seen, had already tracked them in their native deserts,—a missionary Christianity—Christianity in her simplest and most persuasive guise, as the faith of the earnest, the loving, the self-devoted—before they found Christianity in the Empire—Christianity refined and complex, imperious and pompous—Christianity enthroned by the side of kings, and sometimes paramount over them.

The spiritual impressions thus made upon the Gothic races had been well-timed, if we may so express ourselves, in the counsels of the All-wise Ordainer. Had it been delayed till after the Conquest—had they occupied the Empire while yet altogether pagans—while their ears were yet untaught to hearken, their knees untrained to kneel,—they might have rooted out Christianity itself, without giving themselves time to behold, to consider, to respect, and to approve it. The overthrow of the West by the Goths would have been, like that of the East at a later era by the Saracens, the abolition of creed and church and polity together. And such, or nearly such, was the extinction of Christianity in our own island by the Saxons, who of all the conquering races of the North were, at the moment of their triumph, the most completely pagans.

But half-informed, partially converted, mistaken, and ill-trained as they generally were, the Northern nations had already learned at least to recognise a Divine authority in Christian teaching, which made them pause, abashed and awe-struck, at the foot of the rock on which Christ's Church was founded. They paused, like those ancient Gauls in the Roman forum, and admired the venerable image of a spiritual Power, which claimed their submission at the same moment that it tendered them its own. Especially providential it was that at the crisis of these assaults on the centre of the Empire, the place of dignity and power should have been so conspicuously surrendered by the civil to the spiritual ruler. Rome, abandoned by her Cæsars and her legions, was left to the counsel and protection of her bishop and his priests; to the shield of faith, not the sword of violence; to the care of God, not of man. It was to Innocent, to Leo, to the minister at the altar, to the keeper of the Church and the holy mysteries, that the people, stricken and dismayed, had been suffered to betake themselves; and beneath the wing of their spiritual protectors they found security and shelter when the hands of the secular guardian fell helplessly to his side. For between the conquerors and the spiritual ruler—the adviser, the comforter of the faithful—there need be no conflict of interests. The bishops and the clergy might go forth, trusting in no arm of flesh, but in the higher influence of the Holy Spirit to intercede for the lives and lands of their spiritual subjects, for the churches consecrated to God, for the memorials of the departed, for the bones and relics of the saints. They stood erect in the majesty of their office, ministers of God, ambassadors from the gate of heaven. They too, like the invaders themselves, had been once the despised, the injured, the oppressed of princes; they too had been the enemies of Cæsar; they had become the conquerors of Rome in their turn; with them the barbarian and the stranger might sympathize, even as allies and brethren. They made no appeal to arms indeed—to arms they had never appealed; they had clashed no weapons in the face of any assailant before or now—they could rouse no pride, awaken no jealousy. The barbarian came to them with a sword and with a spear and with a shield; but they came to him in the name of the Lord of Hosts only—of Him who had never failed them under tyranny and persecution. They appealed to the spirit within him—to that imagination, that apprehension of the Divine which had been born within him in his native forests—coeval perhaps with the origin of his race; which had been roused by the zeal of Christian missionaries, and kindled to a glow of devotion by the flaming tongues of the Christian Scriptures. They spoke to him of the mysteries of a faith which they claimed to hold with him in common—reminded him of the Captain of his salvation, the Leader of the hosts of angels, the Vanquisher of Satan, of Him who had led captivity captive—and saluted him as Christ's own soldier in the wars of God. They justified to him his career as the instrument of Providence, sanctified his conquests with a Divine title, assigned to him his place in the roll of Divine revelation. No wonder that to the wondering eyes of the barbarians such a teacher taught with authority—that a glory seemed to play about his head, Divine music to breathe from his countenance—that his words were prophecies, his acts were miracles. By all he said and did in that mortal crisis we, in our soberer mood, may set a more legitimate value: the prophecy and the miracle we indeed may discredit, but let us not deride the simple faith which heard the word which was not spoken, and saw the deed which was invisible. Wonders there were which history records and which reason has attested—wonders of providential dealing to which the sceptic may bow, in which the Christian may triumph—wonders of God's protection, of God's judgment, of God's authority. Amidst all the fury and the abounding horror of the barbarian conquests, in the bloody deeds of bloody men on the right hand and on the left, we still find Christianity interposed as a shield between the wrath of the conqueror and the terrors of the conquered. From realm to realm, from city to city, we see the bishop marching with his clergy, singing psalms, addressing invocations, arresting the inundation, staying the plague. Sometimes he prays, sometimes he adjures, sometimes he offers the example of holy martyrdom. And so he conquers his conquerors. The power of his word—the authority of his teaching—is attested by the mercy shown to Rome by the Arian Alaric, when the barbarians cowered before the churches of St. Peter and St. Paul—when they restored the sacred vessels to their rifled shrines, singing hymns to God along with the Roman worshippers—when they spared the city for the memory of its martyred saints: again, in the awe with which the pagan Attila withdrew from the ascent of the Apennines, stunned by the rebuke of the holy Leo, who went forth with crosier and mitre and a single attendant to encounter all the armies of the Scourge of God. Still more the power of the faith was recognised, still more the authority of its teaching manifested, when the conquerors, east and west and north and south, wherever the foundation of the Church had been laid, revered and cherished the Divine structure, maintained its forms, revived its discipline, accepted its traditions, and embraced its creed. Swept over by the tempest, the Church of Christ rose triumphantly again; of all the cities and the races that had obeyed her spiritual law, she lost not permanently one disciple; for this was the Lord's will which sent her, that of all which had been given her she 'should lose nothing, but should raise it up again' in the manifestation of His new dispensation.[1]

Thus the conquerors entered into possession. They gazed more attentively on the imposing fabric before

[1] St. John vi. 39. Notes and Illustrations (K).

them; deeply were their imaginations impressed with the fact of its vast expansion and its claim to universal supremacy. What the great secular Empire of Rome had seemed in ages past, the completion of a grand Divine scheme, Providence revealed, Deity enshrined in an earthly tabernacle; such, with even fuller completion, with clearer lineaments, with power more unquestioned, with claims more emphatic and transcendent—claims on the soul and the conscience—was the faith of Christ, the Church of Christ, the Empire of the spiritual Rome. Her teaching was uniform and consistent; her voice went to the ends of the earth; her language was one, her laws universal. It was the voice of God and not of a man—so clear, so impressive—deep, not loud—convincing, not compelling. Her eyes glanced from earth to heaven; her ears were open to messages from God Himself; so keen her sense of touch, that every impulse from on high vibrated from the heart to the members, every string and fibre of her being was tuned in sympathy and unison. This indeed was the city of God upon earth—the polity of heaven foreshown in this scene of trial and probation—a perfect law enshrined in a perfect temple. For to the rude convert from the North, a child as yet in moral and spiritual training, the Church on earth might seem already perfect. Her defects, her vices, were imperceptible to his gross vision, or seemed in his eyes all complete and glorious rather. Her exaggerated faith, her attenuated morality, her carnal ambition, her spiritual obliquities, all seemed to him, childlike in faith, childlike in obedience, as the tokens of one teaching with authority, to be admired, loved, adored, but never to be questioned.

This triumph of the Church over her Northern conquerors was the greatest, I suppose, of all her triumphs —the issue least to be expected beforehand, most to be admired in the retrospect of any. The vicissitudes of hope, of fear, of despair, of exultation, with which the Christians themselves regarded the conflict, are most interesting and instructive. We, too, in our later age, amidst our own anxieties and apprehensions, may draw from them lessons of hope and faith and reverential submission to the ways of Providence, which are inscrutable and past finding out. Let us cast a glance upon them.

Even in the second century of the Faith, while the Pagan Empire was still standing in vigour almost undiminished—while she repressed the Gospel and trampled on the believers with unshaken confidence in her own might and the right arm of her deities — the Christians, casting about on all sides for hope, for succour, for deliverance, beheld the breaking of a happier dawn in the flash of arms beyond the frontier. To resist the persecutor themselves was against their principles; the Christians must endure, suffering wrongfully; they could but offer the cheek to the smiter, and leave vengeance to Him to whom vengeance belongeth. But could they have invoked the avenger themselves —might they have made themselves allies of the arm of flesh—were there not foes of Rome, enough and to spare, for their deliverance, among the Parthians east, and the Moors south, and north the Goths and the Scythians? Such was their first whisper confided one to another, their first augury of the impending catastrophe. Presently its tones wax louder, its signals clearer, its aspirations more distinct from generation to generation. Not in the grave Apology of Tertullian only, but in the popular verses muttered from street to street, we hear the Goths invoked as the instruments of the Lord's vengeance — as the weapons of the Almighty for the slaughter of an impious generation —to fulfil, with the dire Apollyon at their head, the wrath predicted in the scroll of Revelations. It is with mingled feelings of alarm and triumph that the believers continue to watch the gathering forces of the barbarians before them. The cloud approaches nearer and nearer; the tempest lowers over them darker and darker; the ruin threatened will be general and indiscriminate. Then flies among them from mouth to mouth the awful question: Will God know His own? Will He care to save His own in the universal catastrophe? When He overthrows the Empire, as he surely will overthrow it, will He keep His own Church standing? Will He choose out the sheep from the goats? Will He gather the wheat into His garner? And close on this perplexing afterthought followed the consciousness of Christian degeneracy—of the lukewarm faith, the godless practice, the covetousness and idolatry rampant within Christ's own fold. The Church had preached in vain; she had prophesied falsely; distrust had followed on the failure of her prophecies. The glorious vision of a new heaven and a new earth, which she had proclaimed as the fruit of the conversion of the Empire, and the establishment of Christ's kingdom—where was it? Did the advent of His reign of righteousness appear any the nearer? A new solution offered itself, and men in their agony clutched eagerly at it. The world, they said, was in the throes of mortal dissolution: the End was at hand! Civil wars and foreign wars—plagues and earthquakes—the impending onset of the barbarians;—these were the signs of the End! Already in the third century Cyprian stands appalled before the wrathful faces of the Germans looming obscurely in the distance. From day to day their figures broaden on the horizon. They advance into the foreground. They occupy the whole field of vision. They thrust themselves bodily upon us, and threaten to extrude or annihilate us. They swell into frightful proportions, like the visions of a sick man's dream—like the breast of the mighty monster of the rail, as it bears down boldly upon us, dilating with every pulsation!

When Chrysostom, from the metropolitan throne of Constantinople, beheld the slaughter of a Cæsar in the gloom of a great defeat, and traced the progress of the destroyer by smoke and flame almost to the walls of the capital, he hailed it as a sign of the General Consummation. He remembered the missions he had sent himself to the land of the invaders. The Gospel, he declared, *had been* preached to the ends of the world; the Lord's word *was* accomplished; four ages had elapsed since the birth of the Saviour; an ancient augury was fulfilled. Surely the End was at hand!—Jerome was alone in his cavern in the distance; but to him the rumour of these assaults was carried. He too believed that the World was perishing. 'Everywhere,' he exclaims, 'is there sighing and mourning — the slaughter of the saints, the defilement of God's holy ones. Yet still our stiff necks are not bent; we repent not; we believe not. Through *our* vices the barbarians are strong; for *our* sins our armies are routed and flee! O God! the heathen have come into Thine inheritance; Thy holy temple have they defiled, and made Jerusalem a heap of stones. The dead bodies of Thy servants have they given to be meat unto the fowls of the air, and the flesh of Thy saints unto the beasts of the land.' He was engaged on the exposition of Ezekiel when the rumour reached him of the first attack on Rome, and the slaughter of many of his own friends. Day and night did he sigh for the sufferings of his Christian brethren, and tremble between hope and fear. When at last the capture and sacking were announced, he shrieked aloud, 'The light of the world is finally extinguished; the head of the Empire is stricken down; the world *has* perished in the City!' He groaned in the accents of the psalm of penitence: 'My wickednesses are gone over my head, and are like a sore burden, too heavy for me to bear. Lord, thou knowest my desire, and my groaning is not hid from Thee.'[1] From Ezekiel, again, the prophet of destruction, does Ambrose realize the completion of God's last designs. 'We are standing,' he exclaims, 'by the death-bed of mankind. Famine is mankind's sickness; plague is mankind's sickness; persecution and the sword are mortal sickness. We are gazing on the sunset of the world!'[2]

Yet amidst these gloomy anticipations faith still survived—trust in God's truth and justice survived. There was deep sense of sin and wrath, and fear of a righteous condemnation. Then came repentance and conversion. And these were followed, through God's mercy, by a revival of hope, and confidence unto the end. Augustine, Orosius, Salvian—a new school of Christian apologists—undertake the pious task of vindicating God's providence; of explaining His judgments; of asserting the further purpose of His government, and pointing with calm satisfaction to its progress in the future. In the victorious Goths they beheld the seed of a new race of believers; old names and forms they are willing to discard, as no more instinct with spiritual vigour; they can trace the hand of God still sustaining, guarding, cherishing, producing; life springing from the tomb, and warmth from cold obstruction. Even the fall of the

[1] Psalm xxxviii. 4. [1] Notes and Illustrations (L).

great Roman Empire, the kingdom once of devils, since the kingdom of God and of His Christ—the world-wide polity which brought the name of Jesus and the knowledge of His redemption home to all the civilized of men—even the fall of this all-glorious fabric, after its reign of majesty and power, shakes not their constant mind. They see in it only one forward step in the eternal march of Providence. There is more beyond: revolution on revolution, kingdom on kingdom, like Alp on Alp! New forms, strange faces, are rising above the horizon, and filling, like the clouds around the expected sun, the vault of the eastern sky. God is among them; God has made them and gathered them. Turn to them, and adore Him in them!

Such is the pertinacity of a true Christian faith; such the sanguine augury of those who have taken Christ effectually into their hearts; such the unquenchable hope of the resolved believer. The barbarians, he is convinced, are destined, in God's secret providence, to become themselves God's people; to receive His covenant; to bear His cross with fresher faith, with humbler feelings, more pious and devout, more obedient, more thankful for past mercies, more sensible of His presence and protection, more effective in teaching and example; to raise man upon earth more nearly to the image of the Divine Being in heaven. After all, he argues, why bind the Lord and Ruler of the Universe to one city, to one nation, and one polity? What is Rome to Him, or He to Rome? The heaven is His throne, and the earth

His footstool! He shall found His Church wheresoever it pleaseth Him. Shall not the potter break the vessel himself has made? Shall not the Judge of all the world do right? The old man is dead, and laid out for burial: Behold the new man created unto God, thoroughly furnished unto good works! No! the World was not perishing! No! the End was not yet! No! the City was not the World![1]

How natural and fitting is this view of Providence in the mind of the faithful disciple! He has one conviction, one fixed idea—that his Master's Church is founded on a rock; nor earth, nor hell can prevail against it. No storm can overthrow it, no ruin can annihilate it. Revive and rise again it must after every disaster. In vain do the Heathen rage; in vain unbelief, in vain blasphemy; in vain all the powers of guile or violence, to undo what God has once ordained for ever. We know not what defects it may admit of; what failures it may incur; but blots only can they be, shadows, blemishes; the substance of the Church eternal survives through all changes. She rides out every storm, holds onward over every billow; for heaven is her port, and her pilot the All-wise and the Almighty!

I have read in the records of our Arctic discoveries, how during the long weeks of the outward voyage—while the crew, with little occupation in hand, were divided between regrets for the homes they were leaving, and interest in the strange objects to which they were

[1] Notes and Illustrations (M).

advancing—it was observed that, according to the complexion and temperament of each, they would fix themselves abaft or forward;—the one class, wistful and melancholy, glancing backward on the receding waters; the other, sanguine and alert, gazing with unblenched cheek on the gulfs before them, and scanning with ardent gaze every opening of new incidents and features. Hope was at the prow; at the stern were listlessness and despondency.

Such a voyage and such a crew were no unfit emblem of mortality bound on its venture of discovery to the other world.

The eye of the heathen and the philosopher is ever looking backward. For them the future has no interest. The one sees in the Past his fancied ideal of the good and beautiful, as of blessings gone and never to return; as of youth, vigour and enjoyment, gliding irrecoverably into age and decrepitude: the other scans again and again the lore of ancient wisdom, combines and recombines it, fights over again the word-combats of old, more languidly than before, and smiles at his own illusions in seeking to elicit new truths from the elements of exhausted speculation. Does he venture to imagine, proud and daring in his auguries, that man is still advancing in his moral progress—that the world is getting better or wiser as it grows older? Yet for what purpose? to what end is all this waste of moral power, which has done so little for us here, and has no object hereafter? So the Pagan and the Philosopher sit moodily at the stern, and cast reverted glances on the Vestiges of Creation, and the Antiquity of Man.

But the believer plants himself at the prow. The waters open before him. He cleaves the present, and clutches at the future; wings grow to his ancles; power issues from his hands. He holds on to an untracked shore; fills in his chart with unwavering lines: fresh in hope, buoyant in imagination, he usurps the land of his cherished desire, the land of promise, the land of milk and honey, the home and habitation of his Lord! In every wave around him, in every shred of spray foamed from the billows, he marks an incident of providential guidance, all tending to one mighty purpose, to an eternal and ineffable fulfilment. He too has had his fears and disappointments: he too is human, and partakes of the cup of humanity, the cup of troubles and perplexities: but Faith, Hope, and Love have raised him above his distresses; he has dashed them lightly from his spirit, as he shakes the moisture from his hair.

This hopefulness, so natural and fitting to the Christian, has ever been a note of the Church of Christ. It has been often mistrusted and misinterpreted. The World has often been angered by it. The World said of the early Church: These men are traitors, and would be rebels; they hate the Empire, and are ready to betray it; they love our enemies, and are eager to comfort and abet them:—for the World knew not what spirit they were of: it was a stranger and entered not into their joy. It expected them to despair of the future, and lo! they had hope of the future! It required them to curse the barbarians, and lo! they blessed the barbarians!

And so it has been often in later times, when the Church has recognized her mission in accepting changes terrible to the world, but full of consolation to herself; when she has joined herself to reversals of policy, and claimed her own in revolutions of opinion. And so, finally, may it ever be with us! May the trials of our faith become the seed of faith in those who witness it! Are we harassed ourselves with new forms of thought, new questions, moral and spiritual? Let us cherish the simple faith, the guileless hearts, of the millions around us. Are we threatened with the loss of a province here? Let us gain an empire on the continent of America or Australia, in the isles beneath the Southern Cross. To the common conscience of man the words of Christ, the holiness of the Holy One, will still speak with power. He will always teach with authority. No terror or disaster can ever frown on the Church again more appalling than the onset of the barbarians. No peril was ever more wonderfully averted; no evil more conspicuously turned to good; no insult to God's majesty more gloriously transfigured to His honour.

LECTURE VII.

THE NORTHERN SENSE OF PERSONAL RELATION TO GOD.

Ephesians iv. 13.

Till we all come in the unity of the Faith, and of the knowledge of the Son of God, unto a perfect man, unto the measure of the stature of the fulness of Christ.

The sentence before us, interpreted by Scripture generally, declares the principle of the Christian covenant: that one universal Church is appointed to preserve, under divine guidance, the true knowledge of the Faith, and of Him in whom we believe, the Son of God; and at the same time that this economy is directed to God's eternal purpose of sanctifying the individual believer, with a view to his justification and perfection hereafter. God has made a covenant with His Church in general, in order to carry out His covenant with each member of it in particular. His Church is ordained; it is informed with all necessary knowledge; it is protected and perpetuated: but this is not the end of His covenant. It is the means to the end, and the end respects the individual believer—me and you—every soul that believeth—

every one of us from the least even to the greatest;—till we all come in the unity of the Faith, and of the knowledge of the Son of God,—that is, in the body of the Church keeping for us the Truth and teaching us,—unto a perfect man; unto the highest point of Christian holiness here attainable, to be increased hereafter even to the measure of the stature of the fulness of Christ, our model, our standard of holiness, here at least unattainable.

I spoke at our last meeting of the touching hopefulness of the Christian Church in the depths of depression and perplexity. That hope, which is a special grace of the Christian character — which fulfils a duty and has promise of a reward—was shown forth strikingly in the crisis of the Northern invasions. It was founded on the conviction of faith, that the Lord would not fail His own, the Holy Spirit of God never leave His work unfinished. But not the less did it look, with the instinct of self-preservation, to every human source of confidence, and seek anxiously for every means of realizing its assurance. The Church worked earnestly and circumspectly in building up her converts in the unity of the Faith, and of the knowledge of the Son of God. She exerted herself to the utmost; she strained, no doubt, even beyond her warrant the claims to obedience and submission which they so generously acknowledged. She claimed to speak with sovereign authority, and promised salvation to her subjects, as if it lay almost in her own caprice to give or to withhold it. She spoke of God's covenant with His children, too much, too exclusively, as if it were a covenant with a chosen people, with the Church or society of the baptized; too little as his covenant with each individual soul that believes. She permitted, she indulged, perhaps she courted, the vain superstitious fancies of her votaries, and allowed them to give to pretended miracles and portents the belief they should have reserved for the witness of the understanding and the conscience. But whatever her defects and excesses, she was constrained throughout by an abounding charity; and neither the authority she claimed, nor the terrors she announced, nor the signs and wonders by which she professed to be accompanied, worked, I believe, so effectually for the conversion of the nations and the salvation of individual souls, as the love which moved the heart of a Gregory at the sight of the young heathens from Britain, the love which impelled a Severinus and a Boniface to spend and be spent in evangelizing the heathens in Germany.

Hopeful, however, as the Church displayed herself in the face of the Northern invasion, she knew not, as it would seem, the ground which really existed, humanly speaking, for the hope with which her Lord had inspired her. That ground surely lay in the spirit of independence and individuality which characterized the races among whom her future was cast. I have shown before how distinctly Religion, in the view of Greek and Roman Paganism, was the idea of a compact of God with the nation, not with the individual. Whatever the future hopes or fears of the worshipper—whatever his notion of a retributive Providence—it respected, in his view, the city he belonged to, rather than himself the citizen. 'God,' he would have said, 'is our God:' so indeed says the Christian, 'Our Father which art in heaven:' but there the Pagan stopped; he did not say with David and the child of Abraham, 'Thou art *my* God even unto the end;' he could not enter, like the Christian, into the spirit of St. Paul's exclamation: 'I thank my God, through Jesus Christ, for you all.' He carried out to its full extent the fruitful idea of a national covenant, placing the root of holiness in obedience to law; in subjection to order; in maintaining the mutual relations of man with man as members one of another; in the appointment of a rule, a polity, a commonwealth whether secular or spiritual. This was the economy, doubtless providentially appointed, which ruled the world, which held the bands of civilization, and of all life, moral and spiritual, at the period when the Gospel issued on its mission. This was the inheritance of ancient wisdom into which the Church of Christ entered, when she was exalted to place and power over the heart and intellect of man. And this inheritance the Church of the Fathers, the Church of Nicæa, the Church of Ambrose and Augustine, accepted as the ground on which she was to build, as the framework given her to fill: for neither was the Church then unconscious of her further mission and deeper principles; of her duty to the individual man, as himself heir of God, joint heir with Christ, to be glorified personally with Him, if first he suffer with Him.

The message of Christ to the individual man may be traced back to the utterances of His Sermon on the Mount, when He called men forth from the cities into the open country, from the conventional forms and habits of society to direct communion between Himself and their own hearts; when He revealed to them the mystery of which the world had so long been ignorant, of their personal relation to a Father in heaven. When His disciples went forth from their last meeting with Him, and began to preach to all nations the tidings of His covenant, they found, as we have seen, some slight glimpse attained, some partial apprehension here and there only, of this spiritual destiny of the creature. The teachers of the Pagan schools, long confined to the mental habits of ages of spiritual darkness, had at last roused themselves at the faint glimmer of light dawning—a twilight peering above the horizon from a Sun still hidden beneath it. The Church and the schools met together; the Church shot forth steadfast rays of spiritual brightness; the schools caught and reflected them from hour to hour with increasing consciousness. The dignity of man, as a spiritual being, an offshoot from the divine stem, became more fitly recognized. The notion of the national compact grew weaker; that of the personal compact strengthened and expanded. We admit that the Pagans of the Empire did conceive a worthier sense of the claims of the slave and captive, as a man, a soul, a spiritual intelligence; a being capable of rights and duties; a child of God as well as a servant of man; an integral portion of the universe, an unit in God's creation, not a mere accident or function. We are not blind to the dawn of mutual love and charity, the acknowledgment of a law of sympathy and mutual help and comfort throughout the races and families of mankind, as members of the household of God; to the hope and augury, faint indeed and imperfect, of a common mansion in heaven, a city hereafter to be revealed of which our homes and cities are types and shadows only.

So much may be conceded to the advance of reason and morality among the Pagans themselves, to the progress of civilization, to the growth of the natural man, which, under God's will and providence, had thus added one cubit to its stature. But this we may remark of the advance of humanity among the Pagans, slight and imperfect as it was, that it lay merely in the indulgence of natural feeling; that it was a relief from the sense of pain and disturbance at the sight of suffering, not the acknowledgment of a duty, not the conception of a principle. The Pagan had no regard, in the exercise of charity, to ulterior issues personal to himself; it was no love of a Creator or a Saviour that constrained him; no sense of duty and obedience to a higher will; no effort to do the task appointed him by God, and so put himself in relation with God. It was no fulfilment of a covenant between him and his Maker; no longing in all he said or did to feel that like Christ himself, he was always about his Father's business. In short, it had no hope of a reward for zealous performance,—no fear of punishment for neglect; and, however we may reason about it, this apprehension of a future account, according to the deeds done in the body, will be ever the most effective instrument for the sanctifying and perfecting of the creature. Thus every question is brought back at last to this—How do I stand towards God? The man is brought face to face with his Master and Judge, to whom alone he owes his Being here; with whom only are bound up all his prospects hereafter. Such ideas as these are Christian, and, I may say, Christian only; the Pagan could not conceive or entertain them. And from these ideas has sprung all that is most distinctive in Christian society and culture, as discovered to us in the history of eighteen Christian centuries. The most marked results of Gospel teaching in the world around us have issued from the individuality it impressed upon the views and conscience of the disciple.

This individuality was strongly marked in the Christian society from the first. The great complaint of the Pagans against the believers was, that they repudiated the supremacy of the State, of common interests, over the man and his personal interests;—that they looked altogether to a sphere of action in which the State could have no concern, Cæsar no part nor lot. By this the Pagans, blind and selfish, were perplexed; they fancied themselves thwarted and aggrieved. The feeling which led man to conversion, to abjuring of idols, to refusing of oaths and unholy obligations, to suffering for conscience' sake, to martyrdom,—was strange to them, annoying, irritating. That the same feeling led to a purer morality, a wider humanity, to justice and charity, to the manumission of slaves, the cherishing of the sick and aged, to a religious sense of marriage-duty and of parental duty;—that it was in fact far more conducive to the true ends of civil polity, than the harsh repressive discipline of the human lawgiver, which gave stones for bread and for fish serpents,—this the wisest of them, at last enlightened by experience, were fain reluctantly to acknowledge. The edicts of Julian and the earnest exhortations with which he enforced them, to imitate the Christians in works of love and equity, attest the results already attained by Christian teaching. But the Pagan still rejected the principle on which these results were founded—the principle of man's personal relation to God, prompting him to seek the promised union with Him by doing His works, by striving after His pattern, by aspiring to the measure of the stature of the fulness of the divine Model. The first ages of Christianity sufficiently established the fact that a new revelation of morality had been made, grounded on this close connection between the Creator and the creature.

But the Christian graces, as we have seen, could not grow unto the perfect man amidst a society which was still half Pagan at heart, which still clung to the idea of a national covenant, of a favoured polity, a divine empire, and regarded church-membership, known by outward signs and professions, as the great sufficient pledge of the divine acceptance. Such was the religion of Christian Rome and Constantinople; of the Latin Church of the Empire, and the Greek; but such was not the religion, not the simple revelation made in Palestine, taught by Jesus, interpreted by Paul and the Apostles. The guests invited were not worthy. Jesus must be accepted by other hearts, and worshipped in other ways. A new element must be infused into the Church, the instinct of individuality, the sense of personal relation to the Almighty. The character of the Northern nations as portrayed to us by its first observers, marks the fitness of those races to be called, even from the lanes and byways, to sit down at the Lord's supper. The German, in his native wilds, was imbued, we are told, with the true spirit of freedom; with thorough independence and self-reliance; submitting to law indeed, but only to law as the word of his own will and conscience; yielding obedience to his leaders, but only as chosen by himself. His position was like that of the faithful centurion; as one under authority, having soldiers under him; but the authority was one to which he was not impressed, conscripted, reduced by brute force; but one which he had accepted and acknowledged from choice and reason, for conscience' and duty's sake.

And thus placed under authority, he gained back, as it were, from the fountain of authority powers and privileges of his own. As a vassal he held of his suzerain;

his obligation, his fealty was personal; not owed to the State, but to the Chief of the State; not to the Law, but to the Judge; not to the Word, but to the Speaker of the Word. Between him and his sovereign, service and protection, faith and favour, were mutual and reciprocal. The compact was between the individuals. It concerned them only, and between them no other power on earth could intervene. To the idea of such a compact the Greek or Roman could not attain, for he conceived no such relation to an earthly sovereign. Patriotism he conceived and felt; of loyalty he had no conception. Patriotism was a Pagan virtue, but loyalty is a Christian grace. And as Patriotism was the classical, so was loyalty the feudal principle—the principle of devotion to the person of the sovereign. Four centuries of empire could not engender the feeling of loyalty to the Pagan Emperors; even under Christian teaching the progress of such a feeling was slow and dubious at Rome or Constantinople. But the conquerors from the North brought it with them straight from their deserts, and accepted gratefully the sanction which Christianity seemed so willingly to extend to it. Christianity interpreted to them their own instinct, hallowed their own principle, established and perfected their own law.

For this is the very type, as it seems to me, of the relation of the believer to God, as revealed in the Gospel,—a relation of reciprocal obligations with which the stranger intermeddleth not. To his Lord the Christian must stand or fall. The believer has entered into covenant with his Lord; he is placed in His Church or spiritual kingdom by baptism; his allegiance is claimed, in theory, by virtue of a personal act of faith and submission; a promise is made or implied on his Lord's part in return for this act of fealty, a promise of grace and spiritual protection, a promise of future acceptance. Thenceforth if our heart condemn us not we have confidence towards God. And whatsoever we ask we receive of Him, because we keep His commandments. We seek to know His will, and are earnest in doing it. We attend Him in His courts; we wait upon His appearance; we bend the knee, and open the lips, and pour forth the heart before Him. We press towards Him amidst the infinite multitude of our fellow-subjects; we arrange among one another the times and seasons and ways and means of approaching Him. We have, indeed, our common rules and forms of service; our ceremonial, our etiquette; but these are but outward tokens, adopted for convenience' sake; the true service is that of the individual only, the willing heart, the active hand, the convinced understanding. Each of us has his own grace and acceptance to ask for. To this none can help us but ourselves only. For this we seek each in turn an interview with the Great One, the Holy One. To each He vouchsafes, not charily, not grudgingly, not at stated times and places only, but ever and everywhere, His presence. To each He offers His hand for adoration, opens His lips with favour, admits our claim upon His promise, and sends us home rejoicing. Christ is the type of Christian sovereignty.

And this sense of a personal relation to God, superior to all national and social relations, has produced the highest development of spiritual life in man; of that spiritual life which may lead hereafter to the measure of the stature of the fulness of Christ. The devotion of martyrs, the resignation of sufferers, the self-renunciation of monks and anchorites, the zeal of missionaries, the fervour of teachers and preachers,—all these have sprung from this paramount sense of a direct relation to God, of communion with Him. Such a sense, excited and inflamed to the uttermost, may lead to excess and fanaticism, but its root lies deep in a true Christian faith. It is the fount of a divine revelation. It shows that God has been busy with us, that He has planted, through His Spirit, a new principle of action in our hearts. The old world had its merits and produced its proper fruits, but these are not of them. If here and there we have remarked the shadow of such Christian graces among the later Pagans, they have been remarkable only because they were so rare, so exceptional. Living unto God consciously and avowedly from a sense of love towards Him, faith in Him, hope in Him,—these are fruits of Christianity; fruits, I repeat, of the true Christian sense of personal relation to Him.

Then mark what immediately follows. The sense of relation to God, and to Him only, cannot be satisfied in this life. It claims a further existence, a new life hereafter; it claims union with this Being who is the end of its existence here. It demands Immortality. The Northern nations, to whom the great ideas of Christianity came so closely home, demanded Immortality. The religion of the Germans and the Goths was instinct with a sense of future existence; not a languid hope, a curious speculation, such as might here and there amuse the Greeks and Romans, but a passion, an appetite, a demand, a faith. Hence their souls were 'capable of death,' they disdained to 'spare a life so soon to be recovered.' And as claimants to immortality they joined themselves to Christianity and identified themselves with it. They took it to their hearts; they incorporated it with their very being, made it the spring and life of all their actions, of their going out and their coming in, of their down-sitting and their up-rising. They fastened themselves upon it, as the living answer to every doubt, the solution of every perplexity. When the missionary Paulinus appeared before the king of Northumbria, the cross in his hand, preaching Jesus Christ and the Resurrection, the chiefs met thoughtfully together to listen to his message, and to consider of their answer. Then spake out one of the wisest and holiest among them, and said, as the ancient chronicles have related: 'Man's life, O king, seems to me like the flight of a swallow when it enters your Hall at one door and presently flies out at another. Without are cold and darkness, within the fire burns brightly on the hearth, the lights blaze on the table, the air is redolent of wine and viands, the voice of the minstrel carols pleasantly. For a moment it rejoices in our warmth, our light, and our mirth; in another moment it is gone, and flits from darkness again into darkness. Can this stranger give us sure knowledge of our past and our future, of the dark behind us and the dark before us, let us receive him gladly and entertain him gratefully.'[1]

And such knowledge the preacher of the Faith professed to give with clearness and certainty. The nation accepted and believed it. They felt it as an assurance of their personal relation to God; of their oneness with Him from whom they had issued, and to whom they should return. To this belief they clung with a perfect conviction. With this engrossing belief in immortality all the strength and all the weakness of medieval faith, its religion and its superstition, were equally connected. It admitted of no doubt, no hesitation with them. They found in it no moral difficulty; they followed it to all its logical consequences. In the future life they lived and breathed and had their being. Amidst all their excesses and iniquities, their cruelties and their falsehoods, they still held strictly to the revelation of a future life and a future retribution. This belief they overlaid with many a monstrous fancy; they perverted it to divers fond and foolish inventions; they evaded, with perverse ingenuity, the duties to which it should have strictly bound them. Their visions of Death and Judgment, of Hell, Purgatory, and Paradise, might be

[1] Notes and Illustrations (N).

vain, carnal, and even demoralizing; but they sprang direct from this intense realization of another life, of which we, cold and sceptical as we are, have hardly a conception. How far their belief availed to purify their hearts and curb their passions, who shall say? When I look into my own, I dare not too closely inquire. But there it was; there, deep in their heart of hearts, lay that awful doctrine of a future life and eternal responsibility, ever ready to save souls from the burning, to add unto the Church such as should be saved. Of its constraining force and universal influence take a single illustration. We look with admiration at our monuments of religious architecture. All Christendom is full of them; the history of our faith is visibly written in them. We compare them with the corresponding fabrics of Paganism; our medieval churches with the temples of classical antiquity. I will not ask which are the most beautiful, which express most vividly the religious sense of human nature. But mark how different their origin respectively. The Pagan temples were always the public works of nations and communities; they were national buildings dedicated to national purposes. The medieval churches, on the other hand, were the creation of individuals, monuments of personal piety, tokens of the hope of a personal reward. They were built for the builders' love of God; they sprang from thankfulness for past services, or hopes of future forgiveness. They were tokens of grace bespoken, of sins confessed, of judgment apprehended. They were lifted on high for the glory of God, in acknowledgment of the infinite greatness and power and majesty of Him who once came down from heaven to save them that were lost. Of the thousands of towers and spires that point to heaven throughout this Christian land,—throughout all Christian lands,—each one betokens the aspirations of a believer in immortality; each one may seem to embody to us the upward flight of a spirit, mounting already in imagination to the abodes of everlasting felicity. Again, I say, let us not too closely scan the extravagance and superstition which entered often into the builders' motives. We see in them, at least, a manifest demonstration of the abounding apprehension of a future state, developed by the sense of personal responsibility to God.

But lastly, this expectation of immortality led, and must always lead men, to a practical conviction of the equality of all mankind. He who built a church to God for the salvation of his own soul was convinced of the need of such a church for the salvation of his brethren. All Christians, he believed, had the same interest in the prayers of the faithful, in the ministry of the priest, in the divine sacrifice commemorated within those holy precincts. To build a church was to build up the souls of men, line upon line, precept upon precept, as stone upon stone. He accepted then from his heart the doctrine of Revelation, so repugnant to the heart of stone of the Heathen, that all men are alike in the sight and dispensation of God; that Christ died for all; that 'His father is *our* father,' and 'His mercy is over *all* his works;'

10

that 'in His house are many mansions;' that He 'of a truth is no respecter of persons, but in every nation he that feareth Him and worketh righteousness is accepted of Him.' And so he built his church, that within it there might be no distinction of persons, but that all should have access to God in Christ, partake of the same sacraments, share in the same grace, repose at last on the same bosom.

To so obvious a truth, a doctrine so acknowledged, of the equality of all men in the sight of God, we may feel almost ashamed to refer. But the course of these addresses has, I think, abundantly shown that such a doctrine was not easily accepted; that nothing short of a divine revelation would have discovered, nothing but God's ever-present grace would have practically established it. By the Pagans it was for ages repudiated, and worked its way among them at last slowly, partially, and most imperfectly. The natural Paganism of the human heart, ever ready to rise again within us, as has appeared again and again in history, has long revolted and does still revolt against it. You need not go to books for it. Put aside the records of the past; forget the old philosophers and the old politics, and the old mythologies of which I have so much spoken. Ask of the men you see around you; ask of some adept in physical science whom you may know as one who repudiates the teaching of the Gospel; ask of some moral philosopher, of some statesman, some chief and leader among men—does he hope for a personal immortality for himself?

Yes—he will perhaps tell you, with more or less humility—I do think, he will say, that the feelings and aspirations within me, the gifts of which I am actually conscious here, the greater gifts which I imagine may become mine elsewhere, may suffice to assure me of another state of existence, a higher development in a wider sphere. And so, as we have seen, in their most hopeful mood, said the sages of antiquity. But ask him further:—And have you the same hope, the same augury, for the untutored child, the frivolous woman, the pauper in your village, the sweeper at your street-crossing?—'No!'—he will answer, if he answers honestly. 'No!—No!—I can have no such hope, no such imagination for them; their case, I feel, is very different from mine; their life is not as my life; their spirit not as my spirit; I know nothing about them; I can say nothing about them; I will not think about them, lest the desperateness of their future—for desperate indeed it seems to me to be—should throw a shade of dubiousness on my own.'—So I am sure he would answer; for such was the answer of the sages of old: and the modern sage is no wiser, has no more knowledge of his own than they had.

But ours is a different scheme; a more consistent, a more logical, and, with all its difficulties, I believe, an easier scheme than theirs. God wills, we maintain, that ALL MEN EVERYWHERE SHOULD BE SAVED. He is ready to receive us all, as His children, heirs of God and joint heirs with Christ. And to this point all our teaching tends. This doctrine we proclaim, we enforce, we urge upon mankind, as the last blessed end of the divine dispensation. This is the heart's core of our sermons; this the idea of our ministry and our services. To this the Church is a standing witness. She has borne and still bears her witness faithfully, with no respect of persons, as becomes the interpreter of Christ. We remember how, some years ago, this vast city was moved by the pomp of an illustrious funeral. The great captain of the age, the great statesman of our generation, the foremost man, as we proudly said, of all the world, was to be laid under the lofty dome of the grandest of our Christian temples. St. Paul's Cathedral was to be thronged with the wisest and noblest of our countrymen. The streets were to be choked with multitudes of every class and station. Far and near the people were to be swayed by one spasm of sympathetic devotion. God had taken to Himself the soul of one He had cherished and honoured; and the nation, full of hope and faith, was about to commit his body to the ground, to be raised a glorified body in the resurrection of the just. For myself—if you will pardon the reference—I was far away from a scene which I would willingly have witnessed, and borne testimony, among my fellow-Christians, to the mercies and deliverances we have received through him—as on this very day, just fifty years ago! But a simple duty lay upon me. I was required to bury, in his native village, the meanest, the most nameless of Christ's poor. And so, while here the bells were tolling, and the cannon booming, and beneath the vaulted roof the mighty organ pealing, and among all and through all the murmur of human agitation resounding, we received our meagre pageant,—a pauper's shell borne by four paupers from the workhouse,—and bestowed, in our homely phrase, a humble brother in a lonely churchyard beside a moss-grown porch. At the same moment the same service was performed on the one spot and on the other; the same hymn was uttered; the same Scripture read; the same prayers of faith and thankfulness recited; the same token given of a sure and certain hope of the Resurrection to Eternal Life, when the sand was sprinkled upon either coffin, and earth consigned to earth, ashes to ashes, dust to dust. Both here and there we prayed with humble devotion for the accomplishment of the number of the elect, the hastening of God's kingdom, the perfect consummation, both in body and soul, of All that have departed in the true faith of His holy name. And so the Hero and the Pauper were presented together by the Church to their Redeemer. For such is our belief in Christ Jesus.

LECTURE VIII.

THE NORTHERN SENSE OF MALE AND FEMALE EQUALITY.

GALATIANS IV. 4.

But when the fulness of time was come, God sent forth His Son, made of a woman.

IN bringing these lectures to a conclusion, I may be allowed to remind you of the chief points which I have sought to establish in them.

My object was in the first place to point out the essential difference between the Pagan and the Christian view of religion, that is, of man's relation to God. We marked the narrowness of the view, so common among the societies of the ancient world, which confined the range of divine Providence to the objects of this life, disregarding the future life altogether; together with the results which flowed directly from it, the national prejudices and national enmities which it fostered. But the course of thought and self-inquiry, even among the Pagans, began, as we saw, in time to modify this view, to unsettle the grounds of this conviction, and open the heart to wider and more liberal conceptions of the dignity both of God and of man. Then came forth the Gospel of Christ, and offered still wider prospects, established on surer sanctions, illustrated by the lives and preaching of men divinely gifted. The personal covenant of man with God, the future life, with the equal share of all men in its promises and its threatenings, through an act of redemption common to all:—such were the truths unfolded for mankind's acceptance. The tide of opinion gathered in their favour; but it advanced slowly, retarded by fierce passions and selfish interests. Nevertheless, God was with it, and it prevailed, to the amazement of the believers hardly less than of the unbelievers. The Pagan cults were overthrown, the Pagan schools were converted and transformed. The Church of Christ triumphed and became the Church, the acknowledged teacher and spiritual mistress of the civilized world. Long engaged entirely in this mortal struggle, combating error, dispelling ignorance, subduing prejudice, she had had little opportunity thus far of settling for her disciples the exact grounds of her own testimony, the precise limits of her own creed. The age of councils and symbols followed; the age of doctors and interpreters. Athanasius and Augustine, with their learned and laborious fellow-workers, crowned the work of the early Fathers. But the materials with which the Church now worked were themselves, as we remarked, earthly and corrupt: society was decrepit; mankind had fallen into old age; the seed of the ancient civilization was worn out, and ceased to produce its fruit; the vices of Paganism again spread abroad like weeds, and overran the divine vineyard. The evil spirit of unbelief, of idolatry, of selfishness and impurity, if it had been once expelled from the heart, seemed again to have returned, even with other spirits worse than itself, —worse, as the corruption of the best is ever worst,—with the spirits of religious pride, of fanaticism and hypocrisy. Then God appointed a fearful trial of His Church in the assault of the Northern barbarians; in a storm of savage passions, brutal ignorance, and dark superstitions. She trembled, she despaired, at last she prayed, she hoped, she rose again in faith and spiritual strength;—she awed her assailants; she converted them; she made them her own children by adoption. She spake to them with the authority she had received of God; proclaimed to them her mission as the spouse of Christ, the beloved and trusted of her Lord, and claimed their obedience to herself for His sake. She was instinct with the Hope with which He had imbued her, she proved faithful to her mission, and received her reward. And then she set herself to cherish those graces of character in her new disciples which were fittest to lead them to her teaching, and to which her teaching most directly appealed. Medieval faith approved itself in its most striking and characteristic features the express contradiction of Pagan naturalism. It established the conviction of Man's personal relation to God, of a future state and a future retribution, of the equality of all men in the sight of Him who is Himself infinite above all. In asserting and grounding these principles of faith, more clearly, more generally, more enduringly than ever before, the Church of the Northern nations, the Church of the middle ages, the Church of spiritual Rome, finally triumphed. The world was now converted indeed; the Empire, and the world beyond the Empire, issued on its career of Christian development, to be subjected in after times to other trials, and but too certainly to other corruptions. But Paganism—including both the mythologies and the philosophies of the classical world—as a spiritual creed was now finally abolished, through the special fitness of the Northern nations for imbibing the great principles of Christian Theology.

Man's personal accountability to God,—the future life and judgment,—the covenant of God in Christ with all mankind: these three cardinal truths have been established by the teaching of the Gospel in the hearts of the nations from whom we are descended, whom God called out of the deserts to receive the inheritance of His favour, which the ancients had disparaged and debased.

Such are the points to which your attention has been hitherto directed. There remains, as it seems to me, one further point to be considered, on which I shall this day address you: What pledge and security can we find in the character of these same latest converts for retaining permanently the impression they have thus through grace received? What spirit of life abides in them, to maintain the light which has been once shed abroad in their hearts?

Such a pledge and such a spirit I discover in the considerations to which the text is calculated to lead us:—

'When the fulness of time was come, God sent forth His Son, made of a woman.'

The Scriptures of the Old Testament opened with the divine recognition of the importance of the woman in the economy of God's spiritual dispensations. In the development of our spiritual life, in our training for a spiritual future, her share is at least as great as that of the man. Her part in the Fall, in the sin, in the disobedience against God, in the denial of His Providence and Judgment, have been as great at least as that of the man. She stands in God's first revelation of His love and justice, on the same line with man her partner. She was placed in the same state of favour, and falls under the same condemnation.—Again, God's second dispensation opens with the recognition of the importance of the woman. She is chosen to be the instrument of blessing. She receives the honour, which is above all honours, of becoming the channel of divine grace, as she had before drawn down divine retribution. Jesus Christ, the Son of God, takes the form of man to teach and preach and suffer, as was required of Him; but He takes that form through the woman; and thus for ever seals with the most glorious and irrefragable sanction, the equality of the woman with the man in God's spiritual economy. Henceforth all we have said of the common claims of man one with another,—of the mercies of God—the decrees of God, the providences of God being extended equally to all men, rich and poor, bond and free, Greek and barbarian,—all that the Gospel proclaimed, and the temples and the schools denied or so grudgingly admitted,—must be carried out to their full extent, and applied to the woman also. Reason and logic require it. Do not our own hearts respond to the appeal, and accept it? Do we make any difficulty in acknowledging the equality of the woman with the man in the sight of the universal Father? of the Creator, the Redeemer, and the Sanctifier? Is not such a doctrine generally understood among us as a thing of course? Who dreams of questioning it? Do we not rather scorn and reprove the pretended revelations of heathenism, which have so commonly denied or disregarded this essential equality, and robbed woman of her crown of spiritual glory?

But if this be the case, let us ask ourselves, to what do we owe this conviction in which we are so well agreed? Do not leap to the conclusion that, because it seems so reasonable, so natural to us, it is really natural, and grows up spontaneously in the human heart. No: we require to be led to it, to have it confirmed and sealed to us by divine teaching; we have drawn it from a source of divine inspiration, we have maintained it by the study of the divine Word. It seeks to make a lodgment in the heart that has been prepared and opened for it. It is a seed which will hardly ripen wherever it is casually dropped; the soil must be dug for it, and the germ be tended and watered. And then, with God's blessing, it will spring up and flourish, and become the joy and life of the garden, and maintain its scent and beauty in everlasting freshness.

Upon the spiritual state of the woman, such as she was regarded under the highest Pagan culture, I need not enlarge. She was degraded in her social position because she was deemed unworthy of moral consideration; and her moral consideration, again, fell lower and lower, precisely because her social position was so degraded. This is notoriously the judgment of history upon the subject. Most painful would it be, most revolting, to enter into the proofs of it. But this we may remark in passing, that, if we can trace, as I have already allowed, some slight advance of man's moral consideration under the later Paganism, there is no such advance perceptible in the moral consideration of woman. This field of human culture still remains, I think, wholly barren. And accordingly the woman seems to become morally worse, more frivolous, more degraded. The highest results of Pagan teaching have left one-half of human kind untended, unexalted, unadorned. The elevation of women under the Gospel was undoubtedly a new revelation to the Greeks and Romans.

But nothing, assuredly, is more marked and signal than this elevation, this moral advance, of woman under the Christian covenant. The Saviour of man is Himself born of woman. His virgin mother is pronounced blessed. She is deemed worthy of a special revelation. She is visited by an angel. She receives a message from

God. Mary is a second Eve; more highly favoured, and proved by her faith more worthy of favour. And from the first the sex receives a share of her favour. The inspiration of faith shed abroad in her soul is transfused into her companions,—the companions of her Son also,—the faithful women who are ever found most attentive in listening to Him, most patient in suffering with Him, most constant in believing Him, most ardent in expecting His return. The apostles, once and again, waver, dispute with one another, flee from Him and deny Him; but the women never. The women are always faithful, always loving. The men argue with Him and misdoubt Him; the women anoint His head with ointment, and wash His feet with their tears. It was not to the women that He said, 'Could ye not watch with me one hour?'—not to the women that He thought it fitting to exclaim, 'Watch and pray that ye enter not into temptation!' Those holy women, who are set as patterns and teachers to their sex, received from Him no rebuke, evinced, as far as has been shown to us, no spiritual weakness.

And firmly on the Christian conscience has ever been impressed the example of their piety. It has sealed the claim of woman to equal consideration before God, and therefore to common consideration with man. A new cardinal truth, at which no believer has ever cavilled, has sunk deep into the human soul. By the spectacle and the study of the love and faith, the patience under tribulation, the constancy in good works of the Maries and Martha and Dorcas in Scripture, of Monica and

Paulla and so many others, whose names are treasured in the archives of the Church, the views of mankind upon the relations of man to woman have undergone a silent but complete revolution; and, I might add, a new bias has been given to the history of mankind.

The part which Christian women bore in the first diffusion of Christ's truth is familiar to all our minds from the records of the Gospels, the Acts, and the Epistles. Every book of the New Testament plainly attests it. The place of the holy women who believed is fully recognized throughout Scripture; but it is not brought prominently forward; and on that account perhaps it makes the deeper impression upon us. The women of the New Testament take their proper position naturally, without presumption, without reserve. The mother of Jesus is the type and pattern of them all,—the type of true female piety, loving, trusting, accepting, realizing. She receives her faith, but she makes it her own in receiving it. The regard of our Lord Himself for the element of woman's faith in His little Church is sufficiently marked. His preachers acknowledge it with gratitude, and tender kindly greetings to the female members of their churches. St. Peter, St. Paul, and St. James acquaint them with their functions, and lay down rules for their behaviour. St. John addresses an Epistle to a female convert, and opens to the preacher a new province of spiritual direction.

This, it may be said, is remarkable only from the contrast it presents to the position of the woman at the same time among the heathen. Proceed in the history of the Church of Christ, and the contrast will become more striking still. Scholars know how small was the part of women in the formation and maintenance of moral or religious opinion among the Greeks and Romans, and that part was almost wholly evil. Judaism, under the guidance of the Holy Spirit, boding of things to come, had taken undoubtedly a higher and worthier measure of their spiritual capacity, and trained them for their inheritance in Christ. The holy women of the New Testament are the disciples and children of the holy women of the Old. But we soon discover an advance in their type of holiness. The character and object of spiritual insight has advanced in women as well as in men. Their feelings are intensified; their piety, obedience, resignation, more marked; their hopes and aspirations more definite; their devotion more absorbing; their self-sacrifice more complete. They are received into closer communion with man, their fellow-worker, and with God, the author and finisher of their faith. They have a definite place in the Church of Christ, a purpose, a mission. They are become necessary to religion: without woman's hand and heart, the ministry of the Gospel, we feel, would itself be maimed. God looks upon them, as it seems to us, with tenderer love, and prepares choicer blessings for them. Man at least, as we see, has begun to think more highly of them; for to their memory he consecrates more solemn and convincing testimonies. In the early records of the Church we read, from page to page, of the solid work done for her by women. They become the companions of the apostle and the preacher; the stay and comfort of the oppressed and the persecuted; the sisters, the wives, the mothers of the Saints, on whom the glory of sanctity is visibly reflected. They receive the last words of the dying martyr, and treasure up the memory of his rapture, till they are called themselves to martyrdom, and respond triumphantly to the summons. We feel, now first, that their souls are instinct with the same life as ours; their responsibility akin to ours; their future in nowise different. Whatever be our claims, as men, on Christ's covenant, our mothers and daughters have just the same, and no other. They have loved as much, they have hoped as much, they have believed as much: nay, more. What mansion in heaven can be closed against the sisters of the disciples, who suffered fire and steel in the Pagan persecution? Will God veil His love and glory from the spirit of the sainted mother, who by prayers and agonies of supplications constrained Him to convert to His faith her erring son Augustine? The labourer is worthy of her hire. Tertullian, Cyprian, Origen, Augustine, the great doctors of the early Church, all fully recognize the spiritual equality of the woman with the man; all tend to exalt her to a spiritual dignity to which Greek or Roman, matron or virgin, dared not, dreamed not, to aspire. A new era has dawned for her. One-half of human kind has been almost silently advanced to a participation in the dearest gifts of God, to present grace and future glory. This is surely the revelation of New Heavens and of a New Earth!

Of New Heavens! for it is the revelation of God in heaven accepting for Christ's merits the love, and faith, and humble devotion of her who believes in Him whom she has not seen, accepts from the heart the truth even before it speaks to her understanding, serves Him in prayer whom she may not serve by preaching.—Of New Heavens! because it is the revelation of a future place and occupation for her who has been most full of her Lord's business upon earth,—most constant in good works, and most abundant in good thoughts;—of a blessed place of reunion for those who have served God in holy union here, the man and the woman, whose whole strength in their spiritual service has lain in their mutual support and confidence; whose faith and service would have been a mockery indeed, if death and the grave could finally separate them, and consign the one to life eternal, the other to nothingness.—Of a New Earth! for it is the revelation of a state of equal hopes and mutual aspirations in this life; the woman being made the real helpmate and the partner of the man; the strengthener of his faith, the sanctifier of his pleasures.—Of a New Earth! for it is the revelation of Jesus Christ his Saviour, looking down upon him with Divine love and mercy, and bidding him press the loved one to his heart, as one who may be surely his for ever, not as a fleeting gift of this world only; not as a loan, but a possession. Then see how this revelation has been accepted and acknowledged. See the silent revolution it has effected; mark the traces of that simple creed of woman's place in Redemption. From the recognition of the solemn announcement of our text, 'God sent forth His Son, made of a woman,' has flowed the establishment in Christendom of woman's social position, as the mother of Christian souls, the nurse, the guardian, the instructress of their tender conscience. Woman has become the spiritual mother of the children of the Church. To her we intrust the training of their hearts and spirits. We believe that God first reveals Himself to our little ones through their mothers. From the mother's love they first learn to love Him; from the mother's truth they first learn to believe in Him; from the mother's prayers they first learn to worship Him.

But to this position woman has been advanced mainly by the religious instinct of Northern Christianity. You have read, I doubt not, of old, how among the ancient German races their women were held in esteem and honour, such as shamed the corrupt and morbid civilization of the Romans. The woman was the associate of the man in all his gravest concerns. He guarded her purity, he defended her honour; in return she cherished his manly virtues, soothed his cares, attended him to the verge of the battle-field, received him returning from it, unloosed his armour, and staunched his wounds. But neither did he enter into quarrel with his adversary till first he had taken counsel of her, had deferred to her judgment, and inquired of the divine instinct which he believed to reside in her, to which he ascribed a mysterious sympathy with the future. She was his mistress, his priestess, his prophetess. She was the fountain of his religious life and spirit. She was the angel or messenger of God to him. Of the origin of this romantic sentiment, which flowered in medieval chivalry, and imparted a colour to medieval religion, there is, I suppose, no account to be given: that it should have lodged itself among tribes so fierce and rude, man-hunters and man-slayers as they were, must be a riddle to us as it was to those who first remarked it. But it was plainly connected with the feelings we have already discovered among them, which led them so promptly to Christianity;—to their deep consciousness of the divine and spiritual; to their sense of responsibility to God, of judgment and of a future life. It was a strong religious instinct which courted the mysteries of the unseen, and sought earnestly for the means of communion with it. And if it led so directly to the acceptance of the Gospel teaching, we shall not err in ascribing it to a special providence, shaping its means in silence to its far-off purposes.[1]

This revelation of woman's part in the divine economy,—plainly written in the Gospel,—preached by the early Church, but sealed more definitely by its full acceptance in later ages,—has become the surest earthly pledge of the permanence of the Christian faith among

[1] Notes and Illustrations (O).

us. It has interested in religion the second half of God's human creation; the half which under no other dispensation was admitted to equal hopes and interests with man. It fills the courts of the Lord's service with another and a greater multitude, with worshippers more willing, more devout, more sensitive as well as more numerous. It does more, much more than this. It attaches to the teaching and preaching of the Faith the sex to which, limit as we may its public ministrations, the private domestic training of every generation must ever be mainly confided. More than this, again; Christianity is a moral training, it is a faith shown forth in practice; and it is from the purity and usefulness of women that we all learn the first principles of moral duty, by which our faith is to be hereafter approved. The divorce of mothers from the moral training of their children was an inherent weakness of Paganism, which made it fall and collapse in the presence of the Christians,—of men brought up themselves by holy women in the fear and nurture of the Lord. It would seem, then, that the admission of woman to a full participation in the rights and duties of religion becomes a pledge of the future maintenance and transmission of its truths. God has not disdained, we may say, to gain Himself human support. The love and mercy of the Revealer secure the triumph of His Revelation. Woman has the will—and has she not the power?—to keep this sacred deposit for ever. It is her charter, her title, her security. It is her pride in this life, as it is her consolation in respect of another. She will not abandon it herself; no man shall take it from her. If she lose it, where shall she look for an equal consideration elsewhere? How long will the unbelieving man share with the woman his spiritual aspirations, whatever they may be? Constrained by God's revealed word, he makes her the partner of his hopes, and rejoices in the constraint: but of this she may be very sure;—we see tokens of it everywhere beyond the pale of Christian belief;—that if man denies Christianity he will straightway deny the spiritual claims of woman. For so he did in antiquity: so do perhaps all existing heathenisms: so threaten to do all modern unbelief and scepticism.

The man then and the woman have the same interest in the Gospel: they have moreover the same stake in maintaining the belief in it. To the woman its denial would be at once a fall from the consideration she now holds among us, in virtue of Christ's descent from the Virgin Mother, as heir of an equal future with ourselves. She would descend again to be a mere plaything of the man, the transient companion of his leisure here, to be held loosely as the chance gift of a capricious fortune: or, to adopt the figure of an old heathen poet, she would be but the sauce or side-dish of nature's great repast. To the man the loss would be as great, perhaps greater even than this. It would destroy the very charm of this life, —a partnership in real joys, real cares, real hopes and interests. It would damp his glowing prospects of a common future with the object of his love; it would unsettle his belief even in the common future of men ; and again steep him in the perplexities of the heathen regarding a future personal to himself. It would shake the very foundations of religion,—dislocate the bands of moral duty, which are now straitened by our early training under spiritual and believing women. To root out Christianity among us, and thereby destroy the spiritual hopes and interests of women, would be to abolish our surest pledges for holiness and righteousness upon earth. For the woman, as our earliest teacher and trainer, is the binding element of moral and religious life among us. The systems of the philosophers, as was said of one of the cleverest and most eloquent among them, are merely sand without lime.

But before we part, one word of warning. While the promises to the two sexes are equal, their hopes identical, each has its own part to play in the advancement of the Truth which is so vital to it. Each is a help meet for the other : each has its proper sphere of action, its own responsibility, in harmony one with the other. 'Neither is the man without the woman, neither the woman without the man, in the Lord.'[1] The woman is impulsive and imaginative in her belief: the man inquires and seeks to understand. When these two elements are duly mingled and attempered, belief is sound and religion is sanctified: when they are confused; God's work in the heart is blurred by superstition on the one side and scepticism on the other.

[1] 1 Cor. xi. 11.

We may trace, I think, much of the corruption of the Church in the fifth century, of which we have been speaking, to the disturbance of this equilibrium by the impetuous zeal, the passionate fanaticism, of the women. It was soothing, no doubt, to the vanity of the great doctors of the Church,—great as they surely were,—to be thronged by these sensitive and enthusiastic disciples; to become their chosen pastors, their confessors, the guardians of their faith and hopes; to be courted by them for their learning, caressed for their eloquence; to be urged to correspond with them on religious topics, appealed to in doubts, relied on in perplexities, surrounded in their ardent imaginations with a halo of supernatural graces. All this we discover already in the Church of the Nicene period, in the Church of Chrysostom, Augustine, and Jerome. It was then, as it has been often since, the bane of sound and sober religion. The letters of St. Jerome to his disciples Paulla and Fabiola, repeat the familiar story of the spiritual influence of man's strength upon the weakness of woman, and again of the reaction of woman's sensibility on the harder fibre of man's understanding. We may be sure that wherever man leaves the use of reason and argument, which are his proper province, in the work of the Gospel, and seeks to direct and govern the weaker devotee through her feelings, her imagination, her impulses easily excited and inflamed, the perversion of his gifts will react again upon himself, and upon the Church of which he is constituted the oracle. The superstitions which stole over the fair face of the early Church were due, it would seem, mainly to the fascinations of female piety thus exerted upon the men who themselves had flattered, fostered, and exaggerated it. And this perversion is ever from time to time repeated. Such is the movement we remark and deplore as rife at this day among ourselves,—the tendency of many among us to pay court to the facile piety of women, to play upon their weaknesses, to indulge and pamper their devotional impulses, to colour or distort the truth, still more, to alarm them with shadows, to amuse them with unrealities. Such is the career of the most restless, the most notorious, the most successful, if the issue may be called success, of the emissaries of Popery in our borders. It is the artifice of deceivers self-deceived, of tempters self-entangled; of weak and womanish men, the dupes of their own flattery, the victims of their own frivolous devices, the captives of their own spear and their own sword. We hear them boast of their Paullas and their Fabiolas; of the converts they have made; of the influence they have acquired; of their hopes for the future, in thus gaining to their side the mothers of the coming generation, the women who shall mould the softness of our children, who shall nourish the Church that is to be. But whatever their triumphs now, have they regarded the inevitable consequence from day to day; the perversion of their own faith, the enervation of their understanding; how vain fancies and gross superstitions will thicken around them; how their creed thus flung at the feet of sensitive and passionate women, will lose its hold on the men who persistently think and reason? If, as I believe, the progress of false doctrine in the early Church, the invocation of saints, the worship of relics, veneration for mere shows and shadows of truth, exaltation of fanciful, eccentric, and pernicious practices;—if all this which still embarrasses us, who cling to the continuity of the faith, and the mission of the Church from the beginning, may be truly imputed to the bowing of strength to weakness, of reason to imagination of old;—so do we not behold now, in our own day, at our own door, the same evil principle at work,—the same moral law, the same Divine retribution,—in the recent elevation to the place of accepted dogma of the most extravagant of human inventions, through the same fatal influence of female superstition carrying away the very men who had flattered it and exulted in it? Their sin has found them out. They have been given over to believe a lie; and, surely such a doom would not have been decreed them, were they not themselves responsible for it. God, we read in the simple words of Scripture, sent His Son into the world, made of a woman. This is the charter of woman's redemption, that the man Christ was born into the world of woman. This is the pledge of woman's equality with man, of the common equality of all humankind in the sight of the Just One and the Holy One. And as such it has been accepted and cherished by man and by woman. It stands as the test and token of a genuine revelation. It puts to shame mythologies and philosophies, and brands the civilization of old as a mockery, a delusion, and a snare. It responded as we have seen, marvellously to the instincts of the Northern nations; it speeded their conversion, it tempered, exalted, and purified them when converted. It has produced an army of saints and martyrs; it has leavened Christendom with a fruitful seed of holiness; it has perpetuated the faith by the mouths of maids and wives and mothers. It has been a golden thread running from age to age through the history of Christianity. And it seems to bear within itself the very principle of perpetuity. We can hardly imagine that the hopes and aspirations it engenders in one-half of our kind, and justifies in the other, can ever be surrendered by either.

But if this text, and others like it, simple, plain, and limited as they are, shall be expanded by a human process of so-called development—that is of fiction—and the blessed but humble mother of Jesus Christ be exaggerated into a divinity; if the masculine Church of the apostles shall be moulded to the imaginations of female votaries; if the men, to whom the power of preaching and teaching is given in it, shall surrender their prerogative of thought, and reasoning, and criticism, to gain themselves a false and hollow reputation, by working upon female impulses and fancies—and of this there is danger elsewhere than at Rome;—then the Church which builds on such foundation will lose as rapidly as it will gain; if the women enter in at the one door, the men will go out at the other.

NOTES AND ILLUSTRATIONS.

NOTES AND ILLUSTRATIONS.

NOTE A. Page 47.

IT can hardly be necessary to enter into proofs or illustrations of the characteristic differences I have marked in the views and positions of the great leaders of Christian theology in the second and third century. The mutual bearing and relation of the schools of Justin Martyr and Clement of Alexandria, of Tertullian and Origen, are well known and appreciated among the students of patristic literature. It is due, however, to M. de Pressensé to acknowledge that I have perhaps nowhere seen them so well compared or contrasted as in his *Histoire des Trois Premiers Siècles*, of which I have made much use in putting my first two lectures into shape.

NOTE B. Page 64.

That Arianism was a real and powerful ally of Paganism in the controversies of the fourth century has been fully recognized by theologians. The similar tendency of the Pelagian doctrine has been put in a striking light by M. de Pressensé, while he admits that the theory with which St. Augustine confronted it had its roots in Paganism also. See a lecture, or *Séance historique* as he prefers to call it, published along with some others, by various authors, in a little volume to which is given the title of *Le Christianisme au Quatrième Siècle* (Genève, 1858), p. 325 :—

'Si nous considérons avant le christianisme et en dehors du judaïsme qui l'a préparé, les religions essayées par l'humanité, nous reconnaîtrons qu'elles se divisent en deux grandes catégories : les religions de l'Orient et les religions de l'Occident. Après avoir débuté les unes et les autres par un naturalisme grossier, à la fois voluptueux et cruel, elles se sont séparées et distinguées profondément dans leur développement ultérieur. L'Orient a supprimé l'élément humain dans le problème religieux, tandis que l'Occident, la Grèce surtout, l'a relevé outre mesure. Le contraste entre le brahmanisme et l'hellénisme est frappant. D'un côté l'humanité est anéantie, foulée au pied, précipitée dans l'abîme de la vie divine, aussi bien par l'ascétisme que par l'extase. La divinité seule a une vie à elle ; tous êtres particuliers qui sont sortis de son sein doivent se hâter d'y rentrer et d'y disparaître. D'un autre côté, au contraire, c'est la divinité qui s'évanouit, l'humanité est mise sur l'autel ; elle est adorée, encensée ; les artistes taillent le marbre pour représenter son image, les poètes s'accordent leur lyre pour la chanter. C'est elle qu'on adore sur les autels d'Olympe, et le Dieu suprême de la Grèce est un héros divinisé. . . . . L'Orient a supprimé l'homme ; l'Occident a supprimé Dieu : il n'y a pas eu pénétration des deux éléments. . . . . La grande originalité du christianisme est précisément d'avoir rétabli la relation normale entre l'humanité et la divinité. Il est la religion de l'*homme-Dieu*, et la personne même de son fondateur est la solution effective du problème religieux. . . . . Cette pénétration de l'élément humain et de l'élément divin qui nous frappe dans la personne du Christ, ne nous paraît pas moins admirable dans toute l'économie de la doctrine chrétienne. L'Évangile, qui est la religion de l'homme-Dieu, est aussi la religion de la grâce et de la liberté. Il les suppose sans cesse l'une et l'autre ; il les affirme avec une égale autorité. . . . . Notre meilleure joie n'est-elle pas de sentir que l'Évangile est d'accord avec la conscience et qu'ainsi notre adhésion a un caractère moral qui la rend légitime? Il convenait que la religion de l'homme-Dieu présentât cette harmonie entre le cœur humain et sa doctrine. Malheureusement la divine synthèse réalisée par elle s'est brisée; l'exclusivisme oriental et l'exclusivisme occidental ont reparu. Je retrouve dans le pélagianisme et l'augustinisme un retour des deux grandes religions de l'ancien monde. . . . . le pélagianisme, c'est l'hellénisme. . . . . d'un autre côté l'augustinisme, malgré tous ses grands côtés et malgré son évidente supériorité, n'a-t-il pas quelque peu subi l'ascendant de la théosophie orientale? Augustin, n'a-t-il pas, sans le savoir, conservé quelques souvenirs de ses anciennes erreurs? La suppression totale de la liberté n'est-elle pas un anéantissement de l'élément humain? Sa notion philosophique du mal nous paraît très-positivement orientale.'

The contrast here presented between the great tendencies of thought in the East and West is interesting and impressive. But it is well to bear in mind with Mr. Mozley, in his very careful and thoughtful review of the Augustinian doctrine of predestination, that the same two tendencies do, for the most part, actually coexist in the minds of most of us, which it is the duty of every one to balance and harmonize. I would direct the reader's attention to the following passages:—

Augustinian Doctrine of Predestination, i. p. 29:—

'The two ideas of the Divine Power and Freewill are, in short, two great tendencies of thought, inherent in our minds, which contradict each other, and can never be united or brought to a common goal; and which, therefore, inasmuch as the essential condition of absolute truth is consistency with other truth, can never, in the present state of our faculties, become absolute truths, but must remain for ever contradictory tendencies of thought, going on side by side till they are lost sight of and disappear in the haze of our conceptions, like two parallel straight lines which go on to infinity without meeting. While they are sufficiently clear, then, for all purposes of practical religion (for we cannot doubt that they are truths so far as and in that mode in which we apprehend them), these are truths upon which we cannot raise definite and absolute systems. All that we build upon either of them must partake of the imperfect nature of the premiss which supports it, and be held under a reserve of consistency with a counter conclusion from the opposite truth.'

ii. p. 48. 'The sense or feeling, then, of Predestination is, as has been shown, both sanctioned and encouraged in the New Testament. But while this is plain, it is also obvious that this is only one side of the language of the New Testament. There is another, according to which all Christians, whatever be their holiness, are represented and addressed as uncertain, and feeling themselves uncertain, of final salvation. They are exhorted to "work out their own salvation with fear and trembling;" to "give diligence to make their calling and election sure;" and St. Paul himself, the great preacher of predestination, who, if any, had the right to feel himself ordained to eternal life, and who said that there "was laid up for him a crown of righteousness," also tells us of his careful self-discipline, "lest that by any means when he had preached to others, he himself should be a cast-away." Indeed, to any one who will fairly examine the nature of this feeling of destiny which we have been considering, and how far and in what mode it is entertained rationally, it will be evident that it is not by any means an absolute or literal certainty of mind. It is not like the perception of an intellectual truth. It is only a strong impression, which, however genuine and rational, and, as we may say, authorized, issues, when we try to follow it, in obscurity, and vanishes in the haze which bounds our mental view, before the reason can overtake it. Were any of those remarkable men who have had it asked about this feeling of theirs, they would confess it was in them no absolute perception, but an impression which was consistent with a counter feeling of doubt, and was accompanied by this latent and suppressed opposite in their case.

'Whether regarded, then, as a doctrine or a feeling, predestination is not in Scripture an absolute but an indefinite truth. Scripture has, as a whole, no consistent scheme, and makes no positive assertion; it only declares, and bids its readers acknowledge, a mystery on this subject. It sets forth alike the Divine power and man's freewill, and teaches, in that way in which alone it can be taught, the whole, and not a part alone, of truth.'

iii. p. 155. 'The characteristic of St. Augustine's doctrine [of Predestination], compared with the scriptural one, is, that it is a definite and absolute doctrine. Scripture, as a whole, as has been said, only informs us of a mystery on the subject; that is to say, while it informs us that there is a truth on the subject, it makes no consistent statement of it, but asserts contrary truths, counterbalancing those passages which convey the predestinarian doctrine by passages as plain the other way; but St. Augustine makes predestinarian statements and does not balance them by contrary ones,—rather he endeavours to explain away those contrary statements of Scripture. Thus he evades the natural force of the text that "God would have all men to be saved," by supposing that it only means that no man is saved except through the will of God, or that "all" means not all men, but some out of all classes and ranks of men. . . . .

'St. Augustine then takes that further step which Scripture avoids taking, and asserts a determinate doctrine of predestination. . . . . But there is no reason why Scripture should not designedly limit itself, and stop short of expressing definite truths; though whether it does so or not is a question of fact. . . . . If Revelation as a whole does not speak explicitly, Revelation did not intend to do so; and to impose a definite truth upon it when it designedly stops short of one, is as real an error of interpretation as to deny a truth which it expresses.'

iv. p. 326. 'Upon this abstract idea of the Divine Power as an unlimited Power, rose up the Augustinian doctrine of Predestination and Grace; while upon the abstract idea of Freewill, as an unlimited faculty, rose up the Pelagian theory. Had men perceived, indeed, more clearly and really than they have done, their ignorance as human creatures, and the relation in which the human reason stands to the great truths involved in this question, they might have saved themselves the trouble of this controversy. They would have felt that this question cannot be determined absolutely one way or the other; that it lies between two great contradictory truths, neither of which can be set aside or made to give way to the other; two opposing tendencies of thought, inherent in the human mind, which go on side by side, and are able to be held and maintained together although thus opposite to each other, because they are only incipient and not final and complete truths,—the great truths, I mean, of the Divine Power on the one side, and man's freewill, or his originality as an agent, on the other. And this is, in fact, the mode in which this question is settled by the practical common sense of mankind. . . .

'The Pelagian and Augustinian systems are thus both in fault, as arising upon narrow, partial, and exclusive bases. But while both systems are at fault, they are at fault in very different degrees and manners; and while the Augustinian is only guilty of excess in carrying out certain religious ideas, the Pelagian offends against the very first principles of religion, and places itself outside of the great religious ideas and instincts of the human race. . . .

'The predestinarian passes over the incomplete perception we have of our originality as agents, because his mind is preoccupied with a rival truth. But this cannot in itself be called an offence against piety; rather it is occasioned by a well-intended though excessive regard to a great maxim of piety. He is unreasonably jealous for the Divine attribute, and afraid that any original power assigned to man will endanger the Divine. He thus allows the will of man no original part in good action; he throws all goodness back upon the Deity, as the sole Source and Creator of it, forming and fashioning the human soul as the potter moulds the clay. It may be said, indeed, that his doctrine, in attributing injustice to the Deity, is inconsistent with piety; but he does not attribute injustice to the Deity, but only a mode of acting which, as conceived and understood by us, is unjust, or which we cannot *explain* in consistency with justice.

'Pelagianism, on the other hand, offends against the first principles of piety, and opposes the great religious instincts and ideas of mankind. . . . . The doctrine of the Fall, the doctrine of Grace, the doctrine of the Atonement, are founded on the instincts of mankind. . . . . These are religious feelings and instincts belonging to human nature, and which can never be eradicated so long as that nature remains itself. The Pelagian, then, in rejecting these doctrines, opposed himself to facts; he separated himself from that whole actual body of sentiment, instinct, and feeling which constitutes the religious life of mankind, and placed himself outside human nature. . . . . The Pelagian, then, or, to take the stronger instance, the Socinian, may appeal to the simplicity and plainness of his system—that it contains no obscure and incomplete, no discordant and irreconcilable ideas; but if he does, he boasts of a religion which is self-convicted of falsehood and delusion, and is proved, on its own showing, to be a dream. . . . .

'In this state of the case the Church has made a wise and just distinction in its treatment of the respective errors of the Pelagian and the Predestinarian; and while it has cast Pelagianism out of its communion, as a system fundamentally opposed to Christian belief, it has tolerated Predestinarianism, regarding it as a system which only carries some religious ideas to an excess, and does not err in principle, or offend against piety and morals.'

NOTE C. Page 65.

St. Augustine holds the highest place among the early Christian teachers as the apostle of a pure and lofty morality. His conception of the nature of God, and of the relations of man to Him, while they abound throughout his writings, are most strikingly shown in the *Confessions*, and in many parts of the *de Civitate Dei*, both of which works were composed after he had developed his views of grace in the controversy with Pelagius. It has been remarked as a curious paradox, that the same theologians who most restrain the notion of human liberty and exalt that of necessity, and who would seem thereby logically to enfeeble the claims of duty and morality, are found in fact to be their most strenuous assertors.

'Il serait curieux,' observes M. Rémusat (*Abélard*, ii. 501), as quoted by M. Nourrisson (*La Philosophie de S. Augustin*, ii. 380), 'de chercher pourquoi toutes les sectes, y compris la stoïcienne, qui n'ont pas été franches sur la question de la liberté, et qui, par là, semblaient affaiblir la condition essentielle de toute morale, ont tendu cependant au rigorisme, tandis que l'opinion contraire a quelquefois versé dans le relâchement.

'La solution de ce problème,' continues M. Nourrisson, 'qui se présente naturellement à l'esprit quand on examine les doctrines de saint Augustin, a été, ce semble, indiquée en quelques mots par Montesquieu.

'"Lorsque la religion établit le dogme de la nécessité des actions humaines," écrit Montesquieu, "les peines des lois doivent être plus sévères et la police plus vigilante, pour que les hommes, qui sans cela s'abandonneraient à eux-mêmes, soient déterminés par ces motifs; mais si la religion établit la dogme de la liberté, c'est autre chose." (*Esprit des Lois*, liv. xxiv. ch. 14.) En effet, supprimez ou affaiblissez le libre arbitre, et il faut aux hommes une discipline approchante des lois qui régissent les corps. Toute la morale se réduit alors à un étroit système de mesures préventives. Car l'énergie humaine ne se manifeste plus que comme une puissance brute qu'il est nécessaire de contenir ou de diriger. De là, en grande partie, le rigorisme du calvinisme et du jansénisme lesquels, on n'en saurait douter, procèdent, par certains côtés, de la doctrine augustinienne de la grâce.

'Mais Augustin ne s'est pas toujours défié du libre arbitre jusqu'à le méconnaître. Les yeux d'abord fixés sur la nature humaine, éclairé par la réflexion avant d'être entraîné par la polémique, il a constaté avec une remarquable sûreté de sens que la plupart des philosophes n'ont erré en morale que parce qu'ils n'ont conçu de la nature humaine qu'une incomplète idée. Ainsi, que tous les hommes désirent d'être heureux, que tous aspirent à un bien qui renferme tous les biens, c'est ce qui apparaît avec une évidence irrésistible. Ni les épicuriens, ni les stoïciens, ni les sages, ni le vulgaire n'ont réussi néanmoins à déterminer la nature du souverain bien, faute d'avoir entendu qu'il y a pour l'homme des biens inégaux; de grands biens, de petits biens et des biens moyens, qu'il est nécessaire de subordonner entre eux. Or, l'âme est le bien du corps, et l'âme qui n'est pas son bien à elle-même, a son bien en Dieu. Effectivement, vouloir être heureux, c'est aimer l'être; c'est l'aimer dans sa plénitude; c'est aimer la paix, et ceux-là même qui se donnent la mort afin de se soustraire aux tribulations de la vie, poursuivent, non pas le néant, mais la paix. Cependant l'être et la paix sont uniquement en Dieu. Ailleurs qu'en Dieu, il n'y a que manque, instabilité, vicissitude. Par conséquent, en Dieu seul se recontre le souverain bien de l'homme. Connaître Dieu, voilà la sagesse; l'aimer, voilà la vertu; le posséder, voilà le bonheur. Et Augustin célèbre avec toutes les magnificences de son langage l'union de l'âme à Dieu, dernière fin de l'âme; laquelle n'est pas absorption, mais acroissement, nourriture et transformation de vie par la vérité par la beauté.

'D'un autre côté, jamais apparemment l'évêque d'Hippone ne

s'est montré plus éloquent écrivain, ni observateur plus sagace, que dans la peinture des passions en général, mais surtout des passions qui nous éloignent de Dieu, et qu'il désigne sous la dénomination générique de concupiscence. Car en quels termes chastes et brûlants ne parle-t-il point de la concupiscence de la chair? Avec quelle finesse, mais avec quel accent de mélancolique repentir n'a-t-il pas décrit les mille impressions qui nous assiégent comme par les portes des sens, c'est-à-dire les tentations du goût, de l'odorat de l'ouïe, de la vue? Ou encore, quel moraliste a scruté plus avant les vanités que recèle le désir d'expérimenter et de connaître, les raffinements cachés et imperceptibles de l'orgueil? Il peut y avoir dans les ouvrages de Platon et d'Aristote plus de système, et ici d'ailleurs, comme presque partout, ces deux génies merveilleux ont, en philosophie, frayé la route à saint Augustin. Mais les chapitres des *Confessions* sont incomparables par l'émotion. . . . . Platon et Aristote sont essentiellement des moralistes de la Grèce antique; Augustin est un moraliste de l'humanité.'

But, in fact, explain it how we may, the religion of grace and necessity is essentially a religion of morality. The religion of freewill is essentially immoral. It is impossible not to subscribe to the account of the immoral tendencies of Pelagianism as given at length by Mr. Mozley (*Augustinian Doctrines of Predestination*, p. 104):—

'Raised upon basis thus philosophically and religiously at fault, Pelagianism was first an artificial system, and next of a low moral tendency.

'It wanted reality, and was artificial in assigning to man what was opposed to his consciousness, and to what he felt to be the truth about himself. The absolute power of man to act without sin, and be morally perfect, was evidently a fiction, based on an abstract idea, and not on the experienced faculty of freewill. And when he followed with a list of men who had actually been perfect moral beings, Abel, Enoch, Melchisedek and others, he simply trifled, and showed how fantastic, absurd, and unsubstantial his position was. Human nature is too seriously alive to the law of sin under which it at present acts, not to feel the mockery of such an assertion.

'The system, again, had a low moral tendency. First, it dulled the sense of sin. Prior to and independent of action there exists a state of desire which the refined conscience mourns over; but which is part of the existing nature as distinguished from being the choice of man. Hence the true sense in which the saints have ever grieved, not only over their acts, but over their nature: for, however incomprehensibly, they have felt something to be sinful within them which was yet coeval with them. But the Pelagian, not admitting any sin but that of direct choice, would not see in concupiscence anything but a legitimate desire, which might be abused, but was in itself innocent. In disallowing the mystery of evil, he thus impaired his perception of it; he only saw nature in that to which the acute conscience attached sin, and gave himself credit for a sound and practical standard of morals, as opposed to a morbid and too sensitive one. The doctrine of perfectibility encouraged the same tendency in the system, demanding a lower moral standard for its verification. And the same narrowness of moral basis which dulled the sense of sin, depressed the standard of virtue. The Pelagian denied virtue as an inspiration and gift of God, confining his idea of it entirely to human effort and direct choice.

'But the former conception of the source of virtue was necessary to a high standard of virtue itself. If we are to rely on what general feeling and practical experience say on this subject, virtue needs for its own support the religious *rationale*, i. e. the idea of itself as something imparted. There must be that image and representation of it in men's minds which presents it less as a human work than as an impulse from above, possessing itself of the man he knows not how; a holy passion, and a spark kindled from the heavenly fire. It is this conception of it as an inspiration that has excited the sacred ambition of the human mind, which longs for a union with God, or a participation of the Divine life, and sees in this inspiration this union. Virtue has thus risen from a social and civil to a sublime and intrinsic standard, and presented itself as that which raised man above the world, and not simply moulded and trained him for it.

'This conception has accordingly approved itself to the great poets of the world, who have in their ideal of man greatly leaned to the inspired kind of virtue. So congenial to the better instincts even of the unenlightened human mind is the Christian doctrine of grace, while disconnected with this ennobling conception, morality has sunk down to a political and secular level. Nor is there any justice surer than that by which the self-sufficient will is punished by the exposure of its own feebleness, and rejected grace avenged in a barren and impoverished form of virtue. Those schools that have seen in the doctrine of grace only an unsound enthusiasm, and have aimed at fortifying the ground of morals by releasing it from this connection, have not improved their moral standard, but greatly lowered and relaxed it. With a dulled sense of sin, a depressed state of virtue, Pelagianism thus tended to the moral tone of Socinianism, and the religion which denies the Incarnation. The asceticism of its first promulgators and disciples could not neutralize the tendencies of a system opposed to mystery and to grace, and therefore hostile at once to the moral standard of Christianity.

'The triumphant overthrow of such a school was the service which S. Augustine performed to the Church, and for which, under God, we still owe him gratitude.

'With all the excess to which he pushed the truth which he defended, he defended a vital truth, without which Christianity must have sunk to an inferior religion, against a strong and formidable attack. He sustained that idea of virtue as an inspiration to which the lofty thought of even heathen times ever clung, which the Gospel formally expressed in the doctrine of grace, and which is necessary to uphold the attributes of God, and the moral standard of man.

Compare M. de Pressensé's statement of the philosophical and moral defects of the same system, and the eloquent apology for Augustinianism which he deduces from it (*Le Christianisme au Quatrième Siècle*, p. 321) :—

'Il est évident que le pélagianisme n'admet pas sérieusement la rédemption ; Jésus-Christ est un modèle et non un sauveur ; il n'est pas même nécessaire comme modèle, puisque la sainteté parfaite a été réalisée avant son apparition sur la terre. Au lieu d'être la pierre de l'angle de l'édifice religieux, il n'est plus que son couronnement ; mais quelque admirable que soit ce couronnement, l'édifice ne s'en écroule pas moins, parce qu'il n'a plus sa base. Oter la rédemption de la dogmatique chrétienne et vous n'avez plus qu'une philosophie ; l'Evangile a perdu toute efficace et toute originalité, et il ne vaut plus la peine de parler de ce qui en reste. Au contraire, la rédemption occupe une place centrale dans le système d'Augustin ; la chute y conserve sa gravité et la rédemption sa grandeur. Le temple a son autel et le Christ-Dieu reçoit l'adoration qui lui appartient. Qu'on ne s'y trompe pas ; le pélagianisme renverse tout, aussi bien la morale que le dogme. A vrai dire, la morale et le dogme sont étroitement solidaires. Le premier principe de toute morale sérieuse c'est l'imitation de Dieu. Le bien est ce qui est conforme à Dieu. Par conséquent, plus l'idée de Dieu est grande, plus l'idéal moral est pur et élevé ; plus elle s'abaisse et se retrécit, plus il diminue et s'altère. La morale est donc compromise par l'amoindrissement du dogme, car le dogme est en définitive l'idée de Dieu, telle qu'elle ressort de la révélation. Le Dieu qui s'est dévoilé à la croix dans un mystère insondable de douleur et d'amour, élève seul l'idéal moral á la hauteur de la sainteté, inséparable elle-même de la charité et du dévouement. Voilà pourquoi toute doctrine qui fait disparaître ce grand mystère abaise misérablement la morale. Voilà pourquoi le pélagianisme substitue à la sainteté l'honnêteté mondaine. On ne nie pas la rédemption sans nier en même temps la vraie charité, celle qui se donne et s'immole pour le Dieu et pour l'humanité rachetée par son sang.

'On nous objectera peut-être qu'au point de vue moral l'augustinisme a des conséquences bien graves, et qu'il porte atteinte à la responsabilité de la créature libre. Nous en convenons; mais nous affirmons que le sentiment qui a inspiré l'augustinisme, même dans ses plus fatales erreures, était profondément religieux: ce sentiment, c'était le besoin ardent de donner toute gloire à Dieu, de prosterner, de courber devant lui dans la poudre la créature coupable. . . . .

'L'histoire d'ailleurs apporte son puissant témoignage à l'augustinisme. Partout où il a prédominé, le niveau de la vie religieuse et morale s'est élevé; partout ou le pélagianisme a triomphé, ce niveau s'est abaissé. Cela est vrai dans l'enceinte même du catholicisme: les partisans d'une morale relâchée étaient des pélagiens; les jésuites fustigés par Pascal appartenaient à cette triste école. Pascal lui-même, St. Cyran, Arnaud, Lemaître de Sacy, et la mère Angélique professaient l'augustinisme le plus strict. Qui oserait dire que dans nos propres églises l'augustinisme, rendu plus conséquent et plus implacable encore, ait tourné au detriment de la piété? Si on le disait, les pierres mêmes crieraient; c'est l'augustinisme renouvelé et aggravé par Calvin qui a trempé ces nobles et chevaleresques caractères de la réforme française; c'est lui qui a inspiré des milliers de martyrs.' . . . .

Note D. Page 72.

The anecdote referred to may be worth relating in the quaint language of the chronicle of Gregory of Tours (*Hist.*, iv. 21):—

'Rex vero Chlotocharius, anno quinquagesimo primo regni sui, cum multis muneribus limina beati Martini expetiit, et adveniens Turonis ad sepulchrum antedicti antistitis cunctas actiones quas fortasse negligenter egerat replicans, et orans cum grandi gemitu, ut pro suis culpis beatus confessor Domini misericordiam exoraret, et ea quæ irrationabiliter commiserat suo obtentu dilueret. . . . Exin egressus dum in Cotia sylva venationem exerceret, a febre corripitur, et exinde compendium villam rediit; in qua cum graviter vexaretur a febre aiebat: Wa! quid putatis, qualis est ille rex cœlestis, qui sic tam magnos reges interficit? In hoc enim tædio positus spiritum exhalavit.'

Note E. Page 79.

The mutual approximation of the Christians and the Pagans in the fourth and fifth century forms a curious chapter in history, and deserves to be more accurately examined than has yet been done. It appears partly in the inveterate lingering of Pagan usages and superstitious feelings among the nominally converted; partly in the social tolerance of differences of opinion on subjects which in other ages of the Church have generally placed an insurmountable barrier between man and man; partly again in the assumption on either side of much of the theological phraseology which is properly distinctive of the two religions, and very strikingly in some instances in the dropping by the Christians of all outward regard even to their most distinctive doctrines. Buegnot (*Histoire de la Destruction du Paganisme en Occident*, tome ii. p. 92 *seqq.*) enters into details on the first of these heads. I transcribe some passages from Châteaubriand (*Etudes Historiques sur la Chute de l'Empire Romain*, 3e partie), which suffice to give a sketch of the others:—

'Volusien, homme d'une famille puissante à Carthage, avoit mandé à saint Augustin qu'un de ses amis manifestoit le désir de trouver un chrétien capable de résoudre certaines difficultés relatives au nouveau culte. Saint Augustin, dans une réponse affable et polie, lui envoie une sorte d'abrégé de la Cité de Dieu.

'Le même Père entretient une correspondance avec la population païenne de Madaure. "Réveillez-vous, peuples de Madaure, mes parents, mes frères ! . . . . Un évêque, un controversiste ardent, saint Augustin, appelle des idolâtres ses *parents*, ses *frères*." . . . .

'Quelques années auparavant, il avoit eu un commerce de lettres avec Maxime, grammairien dans cette même ville de Madaure : Maxime l'avoit prié de laisser à côté son éloquence et les subtiles arguments de Chrysippe, pour lui dire quel étoit le Dieu des chrétiens. "Et à présent, homme excellent, qui as abandonné ma communion, cette lettre sera jetée au feu ou détruite d'une autre manière." "S'il en est ainsi, un peu de papier périra, mais non ma doctrine . . . . puissent les Dieux te conserver ! les Dieux, par qui les peuples de la terre adorent en mille manières différentes, dans un harmonieux discord, le Père commun de ces dieux et des hommes ! " Voiçi le païen qui appelle à son tour les bénédictions du ciel sur la tête d'un chrétien.

'Longinien écrit ces mots à saint Augustin : "Seigneur et honoré père, quant au Christ en qui tu crois, et l'Esprit de Dieu par qui tu espères aller dans le sein du vrai, du souverain, du bienheureux auteur de toutes choses, je n'ose ni ne puis exprimer ce que je pense : il est difficile à un homme de définir ce qu'il ne comprend pas ; mais tu es digne du respect que je porte à tes vertus." Saint Augustin répond : "J'aime ta circonspection à ne rien nier, à ne rien affirmer touchant le Christ ; c'est une louable réserve dans un païen."

'Mais avant ces lettres d'Augustin, on trouve peut-être un monument encore plus extraordinaire de la tolérance religieuse entre les esprits supérieurs : ce sont les lettres de saint Basile à Libanius, et de Libanius à saint Basile. Le sophiste païen avoit été le maître du docteur chrétien à Constantinople.

'"Quand vous fûtes retourné dans votre pays," écrit Libanius à Basile, "je me disois: Que fait maintenant Basile? plaide-t-il au barreau? enseigne-t-il l'éloquence? J'ai appris que vous aviez suivi une meilleure voie, que vous ne vous étiez occupé qu'à plaire à Dieu; et j'ai envié votre bonheur." (*Epist.* 336.)

'Basile envoie des jeunes Cappadociens à l'école de Libanius, sans crainte de les infecter du venin de l'idolâtrie. "Il suffira," lui mande-t-il, "qu'avant l'âge de l'expérience ces jeunes gens soient comptés parmi vos disciples." (*Epist.* 337.) "Basile est mon ami," s'écrie Libanius dans une autre lettre, "Basile est mon vainqueur, et j'en suis ravi de joie." (*Epist.* 338.) "Je tiens votre harangue," dit Basile, "je l'ai admirée. O Muses! O Athènes! que de choses vous enseignez à vos élèves!" (*Epist.* 353.)

'Est-ce bien l'énnemi de Julien, l'ami de Grégoire de Nazianze, le fondateur de la vie cénobitique? est-ce bien l'ardent sectateur de Julien, le violent adversaire des moines, l'orateur qui défendoit les temples? Sont-ce bien ces deux hommes qui ont ensemble un pareil commerce de lettres?

'Synésius, de la colonie lacédémonienne fondée en Afrique dans la Cyrénaique, descendoit d'Eurysthène, premier roi de Sparte de la race dorique: il étoit philosophe; comme saint Augustin, dans sa jeunesse, il partageoit ses jours entre la lecture et la chasse. Le peuple de Ptolemaïde, en Libye, le demande pour évêque. Synésius déclare qu'il ne se reconnaît point la pureté de mœurs nécessaire à un si saint état; que Dieu lui a donné une femme; qu'il ne veut la quitter, ni s'approcher d'elle furtivement comme un adultère; qu'il souhaite avoir un grand nombre d'enfants beaux et vertueux. Il ajoutoit: "Je ne croirai jamais que l'âme soit créée après le corps; je ne dirai jamais que le monde doit périr en tout ou en partie; la résurrection [of the body] me paroît une chose fort mystérieuse, et je ne me rends point aux opinions du vulgaire." (*Synés. Epist.* 97, 105.) On lui laissa sa femmes et ses opinions, et on le fit évêque. Quand il fut ordonné, il ne put, pendant sept mois, se résoudre à vivre au milieu de son troupeau: il pensoit que sa charge étoit incompatible avec sa philosophie; il vouloit s'expatrier et passer en Grèce. (*Epist.* 95.) On lui laissa sa philosophie, et il resta à Ptolemaïde.

'Synésius avoit été disciple d'Hypatia, à Alexandrie. Les lettres qu'il lui écrit sont ainsi souscrites: "Au philosophe. Au philosophe Hypatia." Dans une de ses lettres (et il étoit alors évêque), il l'appelle sa mère, sa sœur, sa maîtresse. Il lui trouve une âme très-divine. (*Epist.* 10.) Il félicite Herculien de lui avoir fait connoître cette femme extraordinaire, qui révèle les mystères de la vrai philosophie. (*Epist.* 136.)

'Il n'est pas jusqu'aux poëtes dans les deux cultes qui ne gémissent de ne pouvoir chanter aux mêmes fontaines et sur la même montagne. Ausone, de la religion d'Homère, écrit à Pauline, de la religion du Christ: "Muses, divinités de la Grèce, entendez cette prière, rendez un poëte aux Muses du Latium!" Le poëte de la croix répond: "Pourquoi rappelles-tu en ma faveur les Muses que j'ai répudiées? Un plus grand Dieu subjugue mon âme."' . . . .

[Ampère, however (*Hist. Littéraire de la France*, i. 249), proves Ansonius to have been a Christian, from the lines 'Sancta salutiferæ redeunt jam tempora Paschæ,' &c. And such is the more common opinion. See Bähr, *Gesch. der Röm. Literatur*, i. 475. But if so, the prevalence of Pagan forms of thought and diction is the more remarkable. Ampère thus qualifies him: 'Ausone, chrétien de fait, est païen d'imagination et sceptique par habitude.' Heyne's remarks on the subject are to the purpose (*Opusc. Academ.* vi. 33): 'Miraberis forte in ista temporum orthodoxiæ severitate, propter *ethnica* illa effata et alia hæreticis propiora non adductum eum esse in malignas calumniationes; at enim duo sunt quæ in scriptoribus istarum ætatum observare licet: primo eos, qui a patriis religionibus ad Christiana sacra transierant, plerumque summis tantum labiis doctrinas recens receptas delibasse; secundo, non valde quæsitum esse de notitiis, quas quisque sibi parasset, placitorum Christianorum, dummodo in nullam quæstionem impingeret, quæ in illa ætate proscripta erat tanquam hæresis.']

'Le temps, comme vous le voyez, avoit usé la violence des partis: les hommes supérieurs, le moment de l'action passé, ne tardent pas à s'entendre; il est entre ces hommes une paix naturelle qu'on pourrait appeler la paix des talents . . . . aussi vers la fin du quatrième siècle, et dans les deux siècles suivants, la tendance que les philosophes des deux religions ont à se rapprocher est visible; la haine a disparu, il ne reste que les regrets. . . . .

'Dans cette agonie d'une société prête à passer, l'assimilation de langage, d'idées et de mœurs, étoit presque complète entre les hommes supérieurs des deux religions: mêmes principes de morales, mêmes expressions de *salut*, de *grâce* divine, mêmes invocations au Dieu unique, éternel, au Dieu *Sauveur*. Quand on lit Synésius et Marinus, Fulgence et Damascius, et les autres écrivains religieux et moraux de cette époque, on auroit peine à déterminer la croyance à laquelle ils appartenoient, si les uns ne s'appuyoient de l'autorité homérique, les autres de l'autorité biblique.

'Boëce dans l'Occident, Simplicius dans l'Orient, terminèrent cette série de beaux génies qui s'étoient placés entre le ciel et la terre: ils virent entrer la solitude dans les écoles où le christianisme avoit été nourri, et dont il chasse l'auditoire; ils fermèrent avec honneur les portes du Lycée et de l'académie des sages. . . . Boëce, chrétien et persécuté, étoit un philosophe; Simplicius, philosophe et heureux, avoit le caractère d'un chrétien.

While such was the mutual approximation of the educated classes among the Christians and the Pagans, resulting in apparent indifference to the essential characteristics of either creed, the mass of professing believers were found to relapse into the grossest superstitions and practices of the heathen. In the fifth century,

Leo, bishop of Rome, deplores the deep corruption of Christian society, and adjures his flock not to fall back into heathenism. The old enemy, he declares, is again stealing in as an angel of light, and is seeking to ensnare the believers. He describes his manifold forms of temptation, and warns the faithful against the instruments he employs. Such are they who promise 'remedia ægritudinum, indicia futurorum, placationes dæmonum et depulsiones umbrarum,' who pretend that all the relations of human life depend on the influence of the stars, and exalt Fate above the will of God and of man. Such men promise to avert every kind of evil. The old heathen cultus, particularly that of the Sun (Sol invictus), had formally entwined itself with the Christian worship of God. Many Christians, before entering the basilica of S. Peter, were wont to mount the platform, in order to make their obeisance to the rising luminary. Here was an instance of the way in which the 'spirit of Paganism' had found means of insinuating itself into the very heart of Christianity. Leo could say, with no great exaggeration, in looking at the moral position of the Roman Christians: 'quod temporibus nostris auctore diabolo sic vitiata sunt omnia, ut fere nihil sit quod absqûe idololatria transigatur.' The weddings of the Christians could not be distinguished from those of the Pagans. Everything was determined by auguries and auspices; the wild orgies of the Bacchanalians, with all their obscene songs and revelry were not wanting. Leo, *Sermo* vii., from Krafft, *Anfänge der Christl. Kirche, &c.*, p. 48. See also the work *de Castitate*, which is perhaps wrongly attributed to Leo. See further Buegnot, *Destruction du Paganisme*, ii 215. 'Saint Pierre Chrysologue, qui fut évêque de Ravenne en l'année 430, s'élève dans son cent cinquante-cinquième sermon contre l'habitude des chrétiens de prendre part aux fêtes païennes qui marquaient le retour des calendes de janvier. Il conçoit bien que l'adultère adore Vénus, que l'homme cruel honore Mars; mais il ne peut se rendre compte ce la faiblesse de ces prétendus chrétiens qui ne peuvent résister au charme des fêtes païennes. Ces pervers adorateurs du Christ répondaient : "Non sunt hæc sacrilegiorum studia, vota sunt hæc jocorum, novitatis lætitia, non vetustatis error." Ils n'apercevaient pas les liens qui attachaient leurs idées et leurs mœurs au paganisme, et qu'ils étaient chrétiens seulement par le nom : "Nemo cum serpente securus ludit; quis de impietate ludit? de sacrilegio quis jocatur?" répondait le prudent évêque de Ravenne.'

Compare among various writers of the fifth century, Salvian (circ. 440) *de Gubern. Dei*, viii. p. 165. 'Quis non eorum qui Christiani appellabantur, Cœlestem illam [i. e. Astarte] aut post Christum adoravit, aut quod pejus est multo, ante quam Christum? Quis non dæmoniacorum sacrificiorum nidore plenus, divinæ domus limen introiit, et cum fœtore ipsorum dæmonum Christi altare conscendit? Ecce quæ Afrorum, et maxime noblissimorum, fides, quæ religio, quæ Christianitas fuit! At, inquis, non omnes ista faciebant, sed potentissimi quique ac sublimissimi. Adquiescamus hoc ita esse.'

But, if these be mere declamatory assertions, a curious fact, indicating even more strongly this approximation of sentiment between the Christians and the Pagans, is recorded by the historian Zosimus. (*Hist.* v. 41.) See the account as given by Buegnot (*Destruction du Paganisme*, ii. 55):—

'Pendant que les Romains attendaient avec anxiété le sort qui leur était réservé [Alaric besieging Rome, A. D. 408], des gens venus de l'Étrurie pénétrèrent dans la ville. Ces étrangers étaient sans doute des augures chassés de leur demeure par l'armée des Goths. Ils racontèrent qu'ils avaient sauvé la petite ville de Neveia (Narni) en consultant les dieux selon les anciens rites, que par ce moyens la foudre était tombée sur les barbares et les avait dispersés : ils offraient d'en faire autant à Rome. Le préfet de la ville, Pompeïanus, cause avec eux, et interroge les livres pontificaux pour connaître la conduite qu'il devait tenir en cette grave circonstance. Quoique les Romains pensassent, qu'il fallait conformer à l'avis donné par ces livres sacrés, Pompeïanus en référa à l'évêque Innocent Ier. Celui-ci, préférant le salut de la ville au triomphe de ses propres opinions, autorisa les Toscans à faire, mais en secret, tout ce qu'ils jugeraient convenable. Ils répondirent que le seul moyen d'obtenir quelque secours de ciel était de sacrifier publiquement et d'une manière conforme à tous les anciens usages, qu'il fallait que le sénat montât solennellement au capitole, et que les sacrifices eussent lieu soit dans cet endroit, soit dans un forum de la ville. Aucun sénateur n'osant assister à ces cérémonies, les Toscans furent congédiés.'

Such is the account of the Pagan historian Zosimus; and he allows that the impiety was not actually accomplished. Sozomenus, the Christian, admits only (*Hist. Eccl.* ix. 6) that the sacrifices were demanded by some Pagans among the senators: *ἀναγκαῖον ἐδοκεῖ τοῖς Ἑλληνίζουσι τῆς συγκλήτου θύειν ἐν τῷ καπιτωλίῳ καὶ τοῖς ἄλλοις νάοις*, and refrains from asserting that the bishop proposed to sanction them. Although in this respect the Christian writer varies materially from the Pagan, he goes beyond him in declaring that the sacrifices were actually performed, which would prove at least the connivance of the Christian authorities.

NOTE F. Page 85.

Ecclesiastical historians and essayists have collected the numerous authorities which indicate the fatal corruption of the Christian community from the third century downwards. I quote, in illustration, some passages from the conclusion of Schmidt's *Essai Historique sur la Société Civile dans le Monde Romain, et sa Transformation par le Christianisme* (Strasbourg, 1853):—

'A côté de l'action du christianisme sur la société païenne, il y a eu réaction du paganisme sur la vie des chrétiens; cette réaction a commencé de bonne heure: elle s'est manifestée encore, et d'une manière plus générale qu'auparavant, après le triomphe extérieur et politique de l'Église. . . . .

'Aussi longtemps qu'elle est persécutée elle se garde du contact funeste avec les mœurs païennes; elle sent plus vivement la nécessité de se distinguer du monde, elle resserre le lien spirituel entre ses membres, et au milieu des épreuves sa foi est plus ardente et sa vie plus pure. Mais déjà, dans les intervalles de repos entre les persécutions, cette vie se relâche; la tolérance tacite dont les chrétiens jouissent sous quelques empereurs devient la cause d'un refroidissement de la piété primitive et du premier amour, et les Pères, affligés de ces retours, rappellent fréquemment à l'Église que c'est pour la châtier que Dieu permet des persécutions nouvelle.[1] . . . . Plus tard, et principalement sous Théodose, quand le paganisme est officiellement supprimé, et que l'Empire jouit de quelques année de paix, la plupart des familles riches et considérables finissent par accepter le christianisme; mais elle apportent dans l'Église les habitudes et l'esprit païens auxquels on renonçait plus difficilement qu'aux cérémonies et aux fables. . . . . Chrysostome peut en appeler au témoignage des païens eux-mêmes, pour constater qu'au temps des épreuves, les chrétiens, moins nombreux, avaient eu des vertus plus pures.[2] Les plaintes des Pères sont unanimes à cet égard; en admettent même que, dans leur sainte austérité, il leur arrive d'exagérer le mal, on ne peut refuser de reconnaître combien il a été réel et grand. . . . . L'amour désordonné des richesses et du luxe est un des premiers à reparaître; sous les empereurs chrétiens il trouve des sources nouvelles dans la prescription légale du paganisme; beaucoup de seigneurs puissants s'enrichent des dépouilles des temples,[3] tandis que d'autres continuent de prélever un impôt sur les sanctuaires, dont ils permettent l'usage clandestin aux colons de leurs propriétés.[4] . . . .

[1] Cypr. *De Lapsis*, p. 182, *seq.*; Euseb. *Hist. Eccl.* l. viii. c. 1; Origen, *Hom.* 25 *in Num.* § 4; *Hom. in Jos.* § 1.

[2] *Hom.* 24 *in Act.* § 3; *Hom.* 26 *in* 2 *Cor.* § 4; *Hom.* 29 *in Act.* § 3.

[3] Ammian. Marcell. l. xxii. c. 4.

[4] Zeno Veron. l. i. tract 15.

'L'effet naturel de ce retour de l'amour des richesses a été un grand lefroidissement de l'amour des chrétiens entre eux. . . . Se rattachant au monde, les chrétiens se détachèrent du ciel et oublièrent les préceptes de Jésus-Christ; . . . on vit reparaître les jalousies, les rivalités, les haines, et plus de cent ans après qu'Eusèbe en constate ce retour, Salvien dut s'en plaindre de nouveau, en faisant avec tristesse la comparaison de la vie des chrétiens avec celle des barbares qui envahissaient l'Empire.[1] . . . . Le goût pour les spectacles de toute espèce, pour le théâtre, la danse, les combats au cirque, mal éteint chez beaucoup de païens convertis, survit avec son ancienne violence à la suppression du paganisme. Au quatrième siècle, les chrétiens courent aux jeux, plus nombreux, dit Augustin, que les païens et les juifs; [2] ils y cherchent un délassement, et n'y trouvent que des leçons de corruption, de luxure ou de cruauté; il en est qui se croient des plus fermes, et qui, à la vue du sang qui rougit l'arène, sentit se réveiller en eux les passions endormies, et succombent à de tristes rechutes.[3] Ils remplissent les amphithéâtres aux fêtes les plus solennelles de l'Église, le jour de Pâques, aux heures mêmes des assemblées du culte. . . . . Les dangers publics, la dissolution de l'Empire, l'approche des nations germaniques, ne mettent pas même un frein à ce délire; après la prise de Rome par les barbares, les Romains, refugiés à Carthage, au lieu de s'affliger de la chute de leur ville *éternelle*, se mêlent avec ardeur à la foule frivole qui se presse aux théâtres.[4] . . . . Quand les chrétiens, réveillés de leur insouciance par le bruit de l'Empire qui s'écroule, demandent avec anxiété pourquoi Dieu les abandonne, les Pères leur répondent qu'ils ne souffrent que des maux mérités par leurs vices.[5] . . . . L'auteur qui s'exprime de la sorte, Salvien, porte ses regards plus loin; il

[1] *De Gubernat. Dei*, l. v. c. 4.
[2] August. *Serm.* 88, § 17.
[3] August. *Confess.* l. vi. c. 8; Chrysost. *Hom. in Matth.* § 6, 7, *et alibi.*
[4] August. *De Civit. Dei*, l. i. c. 32; *Confess.* l. i. c. 7. See also Salvian, *De Gub. Dei*, l. vi. c. 12, 15.
[5] Salvian, *De Gub. Dei*, l. iv. c. 12.

comprend qu'il faut un élément nouveau pour rajeunir la société vieillie; c'est dans les invasions des barbares qu'il entrevoit un moyen suprême employé par la sagesse de Dieu pour retremper les forces défaillantes du monde romain; le paganisme avait entraîné l'humanité dans une corruption profonde, les esprits étaient amollis, les courages énervés, les caractères brisés; le christianisme n'était vivant que dans des âmes individuelles, tout en ayant transformé les relations sociales, mais il ne régnait pas encore en maître incontesté, les mœurs des masses lui résistaient encore. Il fallut mêler à une race devenue impuissante une race plus jeune, pour sauver ce que la civilisation antique avait de durable et grand.' . . . .

The rapid corruption of Christian belief and opinion, which seems to have been thus closely connected with the widely extended resumption of pagan usages and opinions, may be further traced to the prevalence of Pelagian notions, which though denounced from time to time by bishops and councils, became, as they have ever remained, practically dominant in the minds of the mass of mankind. See D'Aubigné, *Histoire de la Réformation du Seizième Siècle*, l. i. § 2:—

'Pélage prétendit que la nature humaine n'est point déchue, qu'il n'y a point de corruption héréditaire, et qu'ayant reçu le pouvoir de faire le bien, l'homme n'a qu'à le vouloir pour l'accomplir. Si le bien consiste en quelques actions extérieures Pélage a raison. Mais si l'on regarde aux principes d'où ces actes extérieurs proviennent, alors on retrouve partout dans l'homme l'égoïsme, l'oubli de Dieu, la souillure, l'impuissance. La doctrine pélagienne, repoussée de l'Église pas Augustin, quand elle s'était avancée sous voile, se représenta bientôt déguisée, comme semi-pélagianisme et sour le masque de formules augustiniennes. L'erreur se répandit avec une rapidité étonnante, dans la chrétienté. Le danger de ce système se manifesta surtout, de ce que, mettant le bien au-dehors et non au-dedans, il fit attacher un grand prix à des œuvres extérieures, à des observances légales, à des actes de pénitence. Plus on faisait de ces pratiques, plus on était saint; avec elles on gagnait le ciel, et bientôt on crut qu'il existait des hommes (idée très-étonnante assurément) qui allaient en sainteté au delà du nécessaire.

'Le pélagianisme, en même temps qu'il corrompit la doctrine, fortifie la hiérarchie; de la même main dont il abaissa la grâce, il éleva l'Église: car la grâce c'est Dieu, et l'Église c'est l'homme.

'Plus nous reconnaîtrons que tout le monde est coupable devant Dieu, plus aussi nous nous attacherons uniquement à Jésus-Christ, comme à la seule source de la grâce. Comment pourrions-nous alors placer l'Église sur le même rang que lui, puisqu'elle n'est qu'une société d'hommes pécheurs, dont il est seul la justice? Mais dès que nous attribuons à l'homme une sainteté propre, un mérite personnel, tout change. Les ecclésiastiques, les moines, sont considérés comme les moyens les plus naturels de recevoir les grâces de Dieu. Ce fut ce qui arriva après Pélage. Le salut, ôté des mains de Dieu, tomba dans la main des prêtres. Ceux-ci se mirent à la place du Seigneur; et les âmes avides de pardon ne durent plus regarder vers le ciel, mais vers l'Église, et surtout vers son prétendu chef. Le pontife de Rome fut en place de Dieu aux esprits aveugles.' . . . .

Note G. Page 100.

Dr. Whateley, in a volume entitled *Lectures and Reviews*, has uttered peremptorily a very grave and important dictum: 'All experience proves that men left in the lowest, or anything approaching to the lowest degree of barbarism in which they can possibly subsist at all, never did and never can raise themselves unaidedly into a higher condition.' At the present day, when the presumed discovery of the vast antiquity of man seems to lead at first sight to the conclusion that his career in the world has been one of slow and gradual ascent from the lowest barbarism to his present partial civilization, it would be well that this subject should be more fully developed, and that efforts should be made to point out clearly the distinction between the moral and material culture of man. It will be admitted that two tribes may be very much on a par with one another in their notions of material comfort, their use of implements, and power over the forces of nature around them, and at the same time may widely differ in their appreciation of moral ideas. It may appear that moral culture is almost altogether independent of material progress. Upon this wide and difficult subject I am not about to enter. I only wish to point out how from the earliest periods at which we can trace the moral ideas of the German nations, a period when their material culture was almost as low as any we read of in history, they were imbued with the very same principles on which the moral civilization of the great Caucasian nations has generally been founded. Among French writers there has been a somewhat perverse anxiety to depress the character of their Teutonic neighbours, and relieve themselves from the imputation of owing any portion of their civilization to the nations east of the Rhine. This feeling has appeared in many ways, among various classes of writers. Among others, M. Guizot has produced in his History of Civilization in France (lect. vii.) an elaborate argument to show that the Teutonic tribes of Cæsar and Tacitus were in every respect the exact counterpart of the Red American Indians, not only in their material resources, in which the parallel may be tolerably correct, but in their religious, political, and social ideas. The Germans, on the other hand, have taken up the defence of their countrymen, and impartial students such as Mr. Greenwood among ourselves, and M. Ozanam, though himself a Frenchman, and not an unprejudiced one, have declared themselves convinced of the soundness of their reasonings.

The examination which this last writer has given to the subject in his *Études Germaniques* (*Les Germains avant le Christianisme*, chap. iii.) may be considered to bear with some force upon the question. I refer the reader to extracts from his chapter on the laws of the Germans, which give, however, a very incomplete view of the argument :—

'Ce combat de l'autorité et de la liberté fait tout l'intérêt du spectacle que nous donnent les lois des Germains. Rien n'est plus pathétique, assurément, qu'une lutte d'où dépend la création d'un grand peuple ; rien n'est en même temps plus instructif. Les alternations dont nous serons témoins nous feront comprendre les contradictions des historiens. Nous verrons enfin, des deux principes rivaux, lequel devait rester maître du champ de bataille ; s'il faut, avec quelques Allemands, reconnaître chez les belliqueux tribus de la Germanie le triomphe et l'idéal d'une même société régulière, ou si l'on peut, comme un grand publiciste français, n'y apercevoir qu'un état violent, comparable à celui des Caraïbes et des Iroquois.' [1] (*Études Germ.* i. 106.)

After analysing the German institutions in regard to person, property, family, and government, the author thus sums up :—

'Les lois de l'ancienne Germanie ne nous sont connues que par les témoignages incomplets des anciens, par la rédaction tardive des codes barbares, par les coutumes du moyen âge. Il y reste donc beaucoup de contradictions, d'incertitudes, et de lacunes. Cependant nous savons assez pour reconnaître cette grande tentative de toutes les législations ; il s'agit de maîtriser la personne humaine, ce qu'il y a au monde de plus passionné et de plus indomptable, et de la faire entrer dans la société, c'est-à-dire, dans une institution inflexible et exigeante. L'œuvre était difficile, mais les moyens ne manquaient pas. Il existait chez les Germains une autorité religieuse, dépositaire de la tradition, et qui y trouvait l'idéal

[1] 'Guizot, *Hist. de la Civilisation en France*, t. i. (lect. vii.), et pour l'opinion contraire, Rogge, *Ueber das Gerichtwesen der Germanen*.'

et le principe de tout l'ordre civil. Cette autorité avait créé la propriété immobilière, et la rendait respectable par les rites et les symboles : ainsi elle fixait l'homme sur un point du sol entre des limites qu'il n'osait déplacer. Elle l'engageait dans les liens de la famille légitime, consacrée par la sainteté du mariage, par le culte des ancêtres, par la solidarité du sang ; elle l'enveloppait dans le corps de la nation sédentaire, où elle avait établi une hiérarchie de castes et de pouvoirs, à l'exemple de la hiérarchie divine de la création. Après l'avoir enfermé dans ce triple cercle, elle l'y retenait par la terreur des jugements; elle lui faisait voir, derrière les magistrats mortels, les dieux eux-mêmes armés pour la défense de la paix publique, qui était leur ouvrage.' (*Études Germ.* i. 146.)

He proceeds to institute a comparison between the principles of German law and those of Rome, of Greece, and of India, which he thus sums up :—

'Ainsi l'unité de la race indo-européenne, prouvée par les migrations des peuples, par la comparaison des mythologies, résulte encore du rapprochement des lois. En Germanie comme à Rome, chez les Grecs comme en Inde, on voit les mêmes moyens de civilisation, ou plutôt tous les moyens se réduisent à une doctrine traditionnelle, où chaque institution s'appuie sur un dogme. Assurément c'est un grand spectacle en des temps si anciens et si voisins des origines du monde, de trouver déjà les idées maîtresses des affaires; les vérités invisibles soutenant les choses visibles, l'État gouverné par la pensée de Dieu, la famille par le souvenir des morts, l'homme par l'intérêt de son âme. Ce sont des croyances bien profondément enracinées que cette inexplicable représentation du père par ses descendants, cette souillure de l'enfant nouveau-né, cette déchéance de la femme, qu'on retrouve au fond de toutes les sociétés antiques. Mais dans toutes on voit aussi les instincts violents qui résistent à l'effort de la loi, et qui poussent les peuples à la barbarie. Partout l'oppression des faibles, l'appel aux armes, et l'homme cherchant la liberté dans la vie errante. On a demandé quel était le plus ancien, de l'état d'indépendance ou de l'état de société. Maintenant je crois pouvoir dire que tous deux sont aussi anciens que le monde, parce que tous deux ont leur principe dans les dernières profondeurs de la nature humaine, qui veut être libre, mais qui ne supporte pas la solitude. . . . .

'Mais l'instinct de la liberté s'était refugié chez les peuples germaniques . . . . Enfin ces caractères énergiques, qui ne savaient pas obéir, mais qui savaient se dévouer, conservaient un reste de dignité humaine, une étincelle de ce sentiment d'honneur que les autres peuples anciens n'ont jamais bien connu, et dont le christianisme devait se servir pour former les consciences, et pour fonder sur l'obéissance raisonnable tout l'édifice des législations modernes.' (*Études Germaniques*, p. 167 foll.)

It would seem that in Teutonic society, as far as we can trace it, as well as throughout the other branches of the Caucasian stem, there prevailed an instinct of civilization which made itself apparent—not, perhaps, by material signs, but in the moral and legal principles on which it rested. This instinct, as far as history enables us to judge, belongs to particular races. In them it is innate, and not acquired; with them it flourishes and developes itself; but even by them it can be but partially and imperfectly communicated to the races which are naturally destitute of it. If such be the fact, it militates strongly against the notion, so popular at the present day, that all mankind are gradually advancing in moral and material prosperity, and that (starting originally from a common depth of barbarism) the leaders in modern civilization are only those races which have had the best opportunities, or been most active or fortunate in the use of them.

NOTE H. Page 103.

I would refer the reader, on the subject of the analogies between the Teutonic mythologies and the Hebrew Scriptures, in the first place, to the full and careful work of Krafft, *Die Anfänge der Christlichen Kirche bei der Germanischen Völkern.* The Edda contains, it seems, many statements which correspond curiously with the stories of Adam's sleep, of the flood, of the ark, and of the rainbow of promise. These statements, he asserts, cannot have been borrowed from the Hebrew Scriptures; they must be referred to a common origin with them in primitive tradition, such as may be traced in the mythologies of various other nations. But, he adds, 'Das, was die germanische Mythologie auf Grund der Eddalehre auszeichnet, ist der geistige Gehalt und die durch das ganze System sich hindurchziehende *religiöse sittliche Tendenz*, durch welche diese Mythologie als eine höchst eigenthümliche Entwickelung des sich selbst überlassenen menschlichen Geistes der *christlichen Offenbarung* vorbereitend *die Wege gebahnt hat.*' (P. 143.)

This tendency he proceeds to examine at length.

But the reader will be more interested in the conclusions on the same subject presented to him by a livelier and, I think, an equally intelligent writer, M. Ozanam, in the *Études Germaniques*, to which I have before referred him. (See t. i. p. 96.)

'Ces indications de la mythologie s'accordent avec celles de l'histoire pour faire descendre les Germains de ces contrées caucasiennes qui virent naître aussi la civilisation persane, voisine de l'Inde, de l'Égypte, et de la Grèce, et qui semblent le premier sanctuaire des religions savantes.

'Mais les religions savantes, le dualisme, le panthéisme, ouvrages laborieux de l'esprit, qui voulurent de l'art et du temps, ne représentent point le premier état de la tradition. Au fond de ces systèmes, il faut chercher ce qu'ils proposent d'expliquer, ce qui est plus ancien qu'eux, et sans quoi les peuples mêmes ne seraient pas, c'est-à-dire, un petit nombre de dogmes qui fixent avec simplicité les destinées humaines. Je crois distinguer ces dogmes primitifs dans la tradition du Nord. C'est d'abord une divinité souveraine dont le nom désigne une nature spirituelle, qu'aucune image ne peut figurer, aucun temple contenir. C'est une trinité qui paraît dans les trois chefs des Ases: Odin, Vili, et Ve; dans les trois personnages divins adorés à Upsal: Thor, Odin, et Freyr; dans les trois noms qu'invoquaient les Saxons et les Francs: Donar, Wodan, et Saxnot. C'est un âge d'or où tout vivait en paix, jusqu'à ce que le crime d'une femme introduisit le désordre et la mort. Ici, peut-être, se rattachent d'autres souvenirs: l'arbre symbolique planté au centre de la terre, le principe du mal prenant la figure d'un serpent, le déluge où la première génération des méchants fut détruite. Le destin du monde roule sur l'immolation du Dieu-victime, qui ne subit la mort que pour la vaincre. Enfin tout aboutit au jugement des âmes, et à l'autre vie sanctionnant les devoirs de celle-ci. Ces peuples violents, qui ont horreur de toute dépendance, conservent dans leurs chants les préceptes d'une morale bienfaisante; ils se soumettent aux assujettissements, aux humiliations volontaires du culte, de la prière, du sacrifice. C'est le fonds mystérieux sur lequel toutes les religions reposent. En ouvrant les livres, en comparant les monuments de toutes les nations qui ont laissé une trace dans l'histoire, on y verrait dispersés, mais reconnaissables, les mêmes dogmes de l'unité, de la trinité, de la déchéance, de l'expiation par un Dieu Sauveur, de la vie future. Les mêmes préceptes y seraient soutenus des mêmes institutions. Ces idées, partout corrompues et troublées, retrouvent leur pureté et leur enchaînement naturel dans les souvenirs de la Bible. C'est là que je reconnais une tradition primitive, un enseignement divin, qui fit la première éducation de la raison humaine, et sans lequel l'homme naissant, pressé par des besoins sans nombre, entouré de toutes les menaces du monde extérieur, ne se fût jamais élevé aux connaissances qui font la vie morale.'

I have pointed to the Gothic conception of life as a conflict, with its bearing on Christian doctrine. This conception follows from the nature of Odin, the greatest of the gods, the father of all, the author of life, of wisdom, and of victory. His great conflict, past and future, was with the giants: but this conflict assumed a moral significance.

'Auch der Mensch wurde gleich von Anfang in diesen Kampf hineingestellt. Seine Bestimmung war nicht bloss, die Natur rings um sich her zu bekämpfen und ihre wilden ungebändigten Kräfte sich dienstbar zu machen, sondern der Mensch sollte auch die von Loki empfangene Mitgift, die Sinnlichkeit, überwinden, und der Geist im Kampfe mit ihr die Oberhand gewinnen. Kampf war also die Bestimmung des menschlichen Lebens. . . . . Daher erhielt das ganze Leben der germanischen Stämme seinen kriegerischen Character. Odin, der Gott des Geistes, der Alles durchdringende und belebende Geist, wurde zum Kriegsgott, dem die höchste Verehrung erwiesen wurde. Er ist es, der den Helden mit kriegerischem Geiste erfüllt. Die auf dem Kampfplatze gefallenen Helden leben wieder auf, da Odin sie wieder beseelt. . . . . Die gefallenen Helden werden nach Walhalla geführt.' (*Krafft*, p. 157.)

The legend of Balder, which is narrated in the various Eddas with some discrepancies of detail, but the Christian significance of which cannot be mistaken, shall be told by M. Ozanam (*Études*, i. p. 52):—

'La puissance des Ases est assurée tant que vivra Balder, fils d'Odin, le plus beau d'entre eux, le plus doux et le plus pur. Rien d'immonde n'est souffert en sa présence; rien d'injuste ne résiste à ses jugements. Mais des songes sinistres l'avertissent de sa fin prochaine. Une antique prophétesse se réveille dans son tombeau pour prédire la mort de Balder. La mère du jeune dieu veut conjurer le sort; elle demande à toutes les créatures le serment d'épargner son fils. Le feu, l'eau, le fer, les pierres l'ont promis:

une seule plante, la plus faible de toutes, le gui, oublié par la déesse, n'a rien juré. Loki la cueille, et la met dans les mains de Hæder, frère de Balder, mais qui naquit aveugle. Pendant que les Ases rassemblés éprouvent l'impassibilité de Balder en lui portant des coups qui ne le blessent point, l'aveugle frappe à son tour: Balder, atteint du trait fatal, tombe et rend le dernier soupir. En vain l'un des Ases descend chez Héla pour lui proposer le rançon du trépassé: l'inexorable déesse veut pour rançon une larme de chaque créature. Toutes les créatures pleurent en effet: les hommes pleurent, les animaux pleurent, les arbres pleurent, et les rochers avec eux. Seule, une fille des géants ne veut pas pleurer, et Balder reste chez les morts.

'Rien ne suspend plus le destin qui menace le monde. Un siècle de fer viendra, le siècle des haches et des épées, où les boucliers seront brisés, où les adultères seront fréquents, où le frère tuera son frère. . . . . En ce temps Loki rassemblera les géants et les esprits des ténèbres. Le loup Fenris rompra sa chaîne, le serpent qui enveloppe la terre se tordra de fureur. . . .

'Alors Odin s'armera; il rassemblera autour de lui les Ases, les Alfes lumineux, les héros de la Valhalla. La dernière bataille s'engagera; mais il faut que les puissances ennemies l'emportent. Odin sera dévoré par le loup. . . . . C'est le moment fatal que les chants sacrés ont appelé la nuit des dieux. . . . .

'Mais cette nuit aura son lendemain. Un soleil plus jeune reviendra éclairer le monde. . . . Tous les maux cesseront. Balder reparaîtra accompagné des fils d'Odin et de Thor. Ils reviendront habiter les palais de leurs pères, au lieu où s'élevait l'ancien Asgard; et là ils méditeront les grandes choses du temps passé et les ruines du Dieu souverain.'

NOTE I. Page 106.

The statements early advanced by Justin Martyr and Tertullian of the spread of Christianity among the Germans are too rhetorical in their character to have much weight.

S. Justin M., *Dial. cum Tryph.*, § 117. οὐδὲ ἓν γὰρ ὅλως ἐστὶ τὸ γένος ἀνθρώπων, εἴτε βαρβάρων εἴτε Ἑλλήνων, εἴτε ἁπλῶς ᾧτινι οὖν ὀνόματι προσαγορευομένων, ἢ ἁμαξοβίων ἢ ἀοίκων καλουμένων, ἢ ἐν σκηναῖς κτηνοτρόφων οἰκούντων, ἐν οἷς μὴ διὰ τοῦ ὀνόματος τοῦ σταυρωθέντος Ἰησοῦ εὐχαὶ καὶ εὐχαριστίαι τῷ Πατρὶ καὶ Ποιητῇ τῶν ὅλων γίνονται.

Tertullian, *Adv. Judæos*, c. 7. 'Etiam Gætulorum varietates et Maurorum multi fines, Hispaniarum omnes termini, et Galliarum diversæ nationes, et Britannorum inaccessa Romanis loca, Christo vero subdita, et Sarmatarum, et Dacorum et Germanorum et Scytharum, ... in quibus omnibus locis Christi nomen, qui jam venit, regnet.'

But the testimony of Irenæus, who lived himself in the centre of Gaul, is undoubtedly entitled to more deference:—

Adv. Hær. i. 10. καὶ οὔτε αἱ ἐν Γερμανίαις ἱδρυμέναι ἐκκλησίαι ἄλλως πεπιστεύκασιν, ἢ ἄλλως παραδιδόασιν, οὔτε ἐν ταῖς Ἰβηρίαις, οὔτε ἐν Κελτοῖς, οὔτε κατὰ τὰς ἀνατολὰς, οὔτε ἐν Αἰγύπτῳ, οὔτε ἐν Λιβύῃ, οὔτε αἱ κατὰ μέσα τοῦ κόσμου ἱδρυμέναι. So also Arnobius, *Adv. Gent.* i. 16:—'Si Alamannos, Persas, Scythas idcirco voluerunt devinci quod habitarent in eorum finibus Christiani.' From this period the fact becomes generally recognised, and is referred to by S. Athanasius, S. Chrysostom, &c. At the Council of Nice, a seat was taken by Theophilus, Bishop of the Goths, or Gothia.

Christianity seems to have been first widely spread in the north by the Roman captives carried off during the disastrous wars of the third century. So Sozomen, *Hist. Eccles.* ii. 6. ἤδη γὰρ τά τε ἀμφὶ τὸν Ῥῆνον φῦλα ἐχριστιάνιζον. . . . πᾶσι δὲ βαρβάροις σχεδὸν πρόφασις συνέβη πρεσβεύειν τὸ δόγμα τῶν Χριστιανῶν οἱ γενόμενοι κατὰ καιρὸν πόλεμοι. . . . πολλοὶ τῶν ἱερέων τοῦ Χριστοῦ αἰχμάλωτοι γενόμενοι σὺν αὐτοῖς ἦσαν, ὡς δὲ τοὺς αὐτόθι νοσοῦντας ἰῶντο, . . .

προσέτι δὲ καὶ πολιτείαν ἄμεμπτον ἐφιλοσόφουν. . . . θαυμάσαντες οἱ βάρβαροι τοὺς ἄνδρας τοῦ βίου καὶ τῶν παραδόξων ἔργων εὐφρονεῖν συνεῖδον, . . . προβαλλόμενοι οὖν αὐτοὺς τοῦ πρακτέου καθηγήτας, ἐδιδάσκοντο καὶ ἐβαπτίζοντο, καὶ ἀκαλούθως ἐκκλησίαζον. Philostorgius specified more particularly the results of the victories of the Goths over Valerian and Gallienus, *Hist. Eccles.* ii. 5.

Ozanam, *Études Germaniques*, ii. p. 22:—

'Mais parmi les captifs que les vainqueurs chassaient devant eux, plusieurs portèrent le christianisme aux foyers de leurs maîtres. D'ailleurs, comment les Goths, enrôlés sous les aigles de l'empire, auraient-ils résisté aux progrès d'une doctrine qui avait gagné les légions, surtout quand ils virent la croix sur les drapeaux, quand enfin quarante mille d'entre eux combattirent pour Constantin dans la fameuse journée qui renversa tout ensemble la fortune de Licinius et le règne du paganisme? L'église des Goths grandit dans l'ombre; on l'a vue déjà représentée par l'évêque Théophile au concile de Nicée. Bientôt après paraît Ulphilas, qui tient un moment dans ses mains toutes les destinées religieuses de son peuple. On ne sait rien des commencements de cet homme extraordinaire, sinon qu'il descendait d'une famille chrétienne enlevée de la petite ville de Sadagolthina en Cappadoce par les Goths, qui la saccagèrent en 266, et que ce fils adoptif des barbares, le *fils de la louve* (Wulfilas), comme ils l'appelaient, était compatriote et peut-être parent de l'historien grec Philostorge. Il évangélisait les Visigoths de la Mésie, de la Dacie et de la Thrace, quand il devint leur évêque vers 348, et se rendit en cette qualité au concile tenu en 360 à Constantinople par les Ariens, qui surprisent son adhésion, sans le détacher néanmoins de l'orthodoxie. (*Sozomen.* vi. 37.) C'est alors que, frappé de la majesté des Césars, il put concevoir le dessein de donner à son apostolat le dangereux appui de leur épée. Deux partis divisaient les Visigoths. L'un obéissait à Athanaric, l'autre à Fritigern. Après une lutte inégale, Fritigern invoqua l'intervention de l'empire; Ulphilas semble en avoir négocié les conditions. Les tribus menacées se soumirent au baptême, reçurent des secours, marchèrent contre Athanaric et furent victorieuses. Depuis ce jour, rien ne résista plus à la prédication d'Ulphilas. Il acheva son œuvre par la traduction des saintes écritures, monument célèbre et resté jusqu'à nous. C'était fixer le christianisme dans la nation que de le fixer dans la langue. L'évêque s'en rendit maître, et la força d'obéir à la pensée chrétienne; il contraignit cette parole sanguinaire à répéter les psaumes de David, les paraboles évangéliques, la théologie de saint Paul. Mais il ne traduisit point les livres des Rois, de peur que, la lettre tuant l'esprit, les récits sacrés ne servissent qu'à réveiller les guerrières de ses barbares. [Waitz, in the prolegomena to his recent edition of the Gothic version of Ulphilas, throws some doubt on this venerable tradition, which we may owe to a sentimental fancy of Philostorgius.] L'alphabet runique, usité chez les Goths, avait suffi à tracer des présages sur les baguettes superstitieuses ou des inscriptions sur les sépultures: il fallut le compléter pour un usage plus savant, et le nombre des lettres fut porté de seize à vingt-quatre. La langue gothique, façonnée de la sorte, prit un singulier caractère de douceur et de majesté. On put voir que les grandes qualités des idiomes classiques ne périraient pas avec eux; et la traduction de la Bible, ce livre éternel, commença la première des littératures modernes. Quand Ulphilas parut, peut-être après une longue retraite, radieux de sainteté, apportant l'ancien et le nouveau testament au peuple campé dans les plaines de la Mésie, on crut qu'il descendait du Sinai; les Grecs l'appelèrent le Moïse de son temps, et c'était l'opinion des barbares "que *le fils de la louve* ne pouvait faire mal."'

Note J. Page 107.

Among the Epistolæ Criticæ of S. Jerome (106) occurs a letter in reply to two correspondents among the Goths, Sunnia, and Fretela, who inquired of him concerning some discrepancies they had observed in the circulated versions of the Psalms:—

'Vere in vobis apostolicus et propheticus sermo completus est: in omnem terram exiit sonus eorum et in fines terræ verba eorum (Psalm. xviii. 5; Rom. x. 18). Quis hoc crederet ut barbara Getarum lingua Hebraicam quæreret veritatem, et dormitantibus, immo contendentibus Græcis, ipsa Germania Spiritus Sancti eloquia scrutaretur? In veritate cognovi quod non est personarum acceptor Deus; sed in omni gente qui timet Deum et operatur justitiam acceptus est illi. Dudum callosa tenendo capulum manus, et digiti tractandis sagittis aptiores, ad stilum calamumque consuescunt; et bellicosa pectora vertuntur in mansuetudinem Christianam. Nunc et Isaiæ vaticinium credimus esse completum; concident gladios suos in aratra, et lanceas suas in falces; et non sumet gens contra gentem gladium, et non discent pugnare.' (Isai. ii. 4.)

In the *Epist.* 57 (107) *ad Lætam* he speaks in glowing terms of the spread of the Gospel:—'Deposuit pharetras Armenius; Hunni discunt Psalterium; Scythiæ frigora fervent calore fidei; Getarum rutilus et flavus exercitus ecclesiarum circumfert tentoria; et ideo forsitan contra nos æqua pugnant acie, quia pari religione confidunt.'

Comp. Athanasius *De Incarn. Verbi*, sub fin. Eusebius, *Vit. Constant.* iv. 5. Chrysostom, *Hom.* viii.

NOTE K. Page 118.

Among both Christians and Pagans the first capture of Rome (by Alaric, A.D. 410) was regarded as the turning-point in the providential government of God. Thenceforth the Pagans could no longer maintain that the the empire was under the special protection of the deities of the old mythology. This point was definitively settled. But, on the other hand, might not the disasters of the empire, now professedly Christian, be supposed to impeach the favour of the God of the Christians? It was the great object of the apologists of the fifth century to parry this conclusion. In this cause they made no doubt many hardy assertions, and uttered some loose declamation; and modern historians have been more or less affected by their personal prejudices in judging of the testimony of facts. I am glad to be able to refer on this point to the summing-up of Mr. Greenwood, whose moderation and good sense are as conspicuous as his diligence. (*History of the Germans*, i. p. 382, foll.)

'It is impossible to withhold our praise from the temper in which Alaric approached Rome. Every precaution was taken to restrict, as much as possible, the bloodshed and destruction which, in case of capture by storm, could not be wholly prevented. It was strictly enjoined that the lives of all who took refuge within the churches, and more particularly within the sacred precincts of the Basilicas of St. Peter and St. Paul, should be spared; and that in the pursuit of plunder the warriors should abstain from needless outrage or vengeful slaughter. It is generally admitted by contemporary historians, that the character of Alaric was not incapable of moderate, or even generous views, and the ecclesiastical writers seem to assume that his conduct on this occasion was at least as much directed by religious and reverential feelings as by resentment, or the hope of temporal advantage.[1] On the night of the 20th of August, four hundred and ten years after Christ, a successful assault upon the Salarian gate delivered the ancient capital of the civilized world into the hands of a barbarian conqueror.[2] No one can doubt that, in spite of the authority of Alaric, and the religious prepossessions of his followers, much blood was spilt, and that very many of those enormities which attend upon a successful storm must have occurred on this memorable

[1] Orosius, vii. 35; Augustin, *De Civit. Dei*, i. 1.

[2] Procop. *De Bell. Vandal*, i. p. 7, edit. Grotii.

occasion; but if the proper allowance be made for the impression the event itself was calculated to produce, and for the character of the assailants, we think the amount of suffering inflicted and endured will be reduced far below what might have been expected. When the first rumour of this stupefying calamity was spread abroad in the Roman world, we naturally expect to find its echo a thousand times repeated, in every form of horror and exaggeration with which ignorant alarm could invest it. And in truth, St. Jerome at Bethlehem, and St. Augustin in Africa, shook the Christian world with fearful announcements of cruelty, and slaughter, and unutterable abominations.[1] It is by no means surprising that these zealous men should have availed themselves to the full extent of the impression such an event could not fail to produce, to reprove sin, to denounce the Divine vengeance against a weak and vicious generation. . . . . But when the true character of the calamity became better known, these good men at once dropped the language of denunciation.[2] Even in the height of unbridled pillage, we are told, the captors religiously respected the churches, their ornaments, treasures, and furniture; the lives of all who took refuge within the sacred precincts were spared; St. Jerome and Orosius adduce remarkable instances of forbearance to their credit, and St. Augustine draws an eloquent parallel between their conduct and that of the Romans.'[3] . . . .

Of the mission of S. Leo to Attila about forty years later, which

[1] See particularly S. Jerome's Letter to Principia (*Ep.* 96, p. 783) and Gaudentia (*Ep.* 98, p. 799). Comp. Augustin, *De Excidio*, &c., c. 2, p. 330; *De Civit. Dei*, lib. i. c. 7; *Opera*, tom. vii. p. 6.

[2] 'Quicquid ergo,' says S. Augustin (loc. mod. cit.), 'vastationis, trucidationis, deprædationis, concremationis, afflictionis, in ista recentissima Romana clade commissum est, fuit hoc consuetudo bellorum.' . . . The whole chapter bears strong testimony to the moderation of the Goths, and expresses Augustin's conviction that it was alone attributable to the benign influence of Christianity.

[3] S. Jerome *Ad Principiam*, Orosius, lib. vii. c. 39; Augustin, *De. Civ. Dei*, lib. iii. c. 29.

resulted in the diversion of the Huns from another attack on Rome, a writer of genius has given a striking picture from materials which, it must be confessed, are painfully meagre. See M. Amédée Thierry, *Histoire d'Attila*, i. p. 206. 'Dans tous les conseils du prince, du sénat et du peuple romain, dit avec une amère raillerie le chroniqueur Prosper d'Aquitaine, témoin des événements, rien ne parut plus salutaire que d'implorer la paix de ce roi féroce. Le silence de l'histoire justifie du moins Aëtius de toute participation à un acte aussi honteux. A la tête de son armée et méditant, selon toute apparence, le plan de défense des Apennins, le patrice s'occupait de sauver Rome: elle ne le consulta pas pour se livrer. Cependant, afin de couvrir autant que possible l'ignominie de la négociation par l'éminence du négociateur, on choisit pour chef de l'ambassade le successeur même de saint Pierre, le pape Léon, auquel furent adjoints deux sénateurs illustres, dont l'un, nommé Gennadius Aviénus, prétendait descendre de Valérius Corvinus, et, suivant l'expression de Sidoine Apollinaire, "était prince après le prince qui portait la pourpre."

'Léon, que l'église romaine a surnommé le *Grand*, et l'église grecque le *Sage*,[1] occupait alors le siége apostolique avec un éclat de talent et une autorité de caractère qui imposaient même aux païens. Les gens lettrés le proclamaient, par un singulier abus de langage, le Cicéron de la chaire catholique, l'Homère de la théologie, et l'Aristote de la foi;[2] les gens du monde appréciaient en lui ce parfait accord des qualités intellectuelles que son biographe appelle, avec un assez grand bonheur d'expression, "la santé de l'esprit,"[3] savoir, une intelligence ferme, simple et toujours droits, et une rare finesse de vue, unie au don de persuader. Ces qualités

[1] πάνσοφος. *Vit. S. Leon. Magn.* ap. Boll. 11 Apr.

[2] Sunt viri auctoritate graves . . . qui Leonem non vereantur appellare ecclesiasticæ dictionis Tullium, theologiæ Homerum, rationum fidei Aristotelem.—*Id. ibid.*

[3] Tanta in Leone tamque mirabilis ingenii facilitas, tanta sanitas, tantaque præsentia.—*Id. ibid.*

avaient fait de Léon un négociateur utile dans les choses du siècle, en même temps que pasteur éminent dans l'église. Il n'était encore que diacre, lorsqu'en 440 il plut à la régente Placidie de l'envoyer dans les Gaules pour apaiser, entre Aëtius et un des grands fonctionnaires de cette préfecture nommé Albinus, une querelle naissante, qui pouvait conduire à la guerre civile et embraser tout l'occident. Léon, arrivé avec la seule recommandation de sa personne, parvint à réconcilier deux rivaux qui passaient à bon droit pour peu traitables, et pendant ce temps-là le peuple et le clergé de Rome, à qui appartenait l'élection des papes, l'élevaient à la chaire pontificale, quoiqu'il ne fût pas encore prêtre, tant ses vertus, dans l'estime publique, marchaient de pair avec ses talents. Depuis lors il n'avait fait que grandir en expérience et en savoir par la pratique des affaires de l'église, qui embrassaient un grand nombre d'intérêts séculiers. L'histoire nous le peint comme un vieillard d'une haute taille et d'une physionomie noble que sa longue chevelure blanche rendait plus vénérable.[1] C'était sur lui que l'empereur et le sénat comptaient principalement pour arrêter le terrible Attila. Il n'y avait pas jusqu'à son nom de Leo, lion, qui ne semblât d'un favorable augure pour cette négociation difficile; et le peuple lui appliquait comme une prophétie le verset suivant des proverbes de Salomon: "Le juste est un lion qui ne connaît ni l'hésitation ni la crainte."[2]

'Les ambassadeurs voyageaient à grandes journées, afin de joindre Attila avant qu'il eût passé le Pô; ils le rencontrèrent un peu au-dessous de Mantoue, dans le lieu appelé Champ Ambulée, où se trouvait un des gués du Mincio.[3] Ce fut un moment grave dans l'existence de la ville de Rome que celui où deux de ses en-

[1] Senex innocuæ simplicitatis, multa canitie. . . .—*Id. ibid.* Lors de la translation de ses reliques on trouva que son corps avait sept palmes trois quarts de hauteur. Il était maigre et extenué.

[2] *Proverbs* xxviii. 1; xxx. 30.

[3] In Acroventu Mamboleio, ubi Mincius amnis commeantium frequentatione transitur. Jornandes, *De Reb. Get.* 42.—Campus Ambuleius.

fants les plus illustres, un représentant des vieilles races latines qui avaient conquis le monde par l'épée, et le chef des races nouvelles qui le conquéraient par la religion, venaient mettre aux pieds d'un roi barbare la rançon du Capitole. Ce fut un moment non moins grave dans la vie d'Attila. Les récits qui précèdent nous ont fait voir le roi des Huns dominé surtout par l'orgueil, et, si avare qu'il fut, plus altéré encore d'honneurs que d'argent. L'idée d'avoir à ses genoux Rome suppliante, attendant de sa bouche avec tremblement un arrêt de vie ou de mort, abaissant la toge des Valérien et la tiare des successeurs de Pierre devant celui qu'elle avait traité si longtemps comme un barbare misérable, employant en un mot pour le fléchir tout ce qu'elle possédait de grandeurs au ciel et sur la terre; cette idée le remplit d'une joie qu'il ne savait pas cacher. Se faire reconnaître vainqueur et maître, c'était à ses yeux autant que l'être en effet; d'ailleurs il humiliait Aëtius, dont il brisait l'épée d'un seul mot. Sa vanité et celle de son peuple se trouvaient satisfaites, et il pouvait repartir sans honte. Sous l'influence de ces pensées, il ordonna qu'on lui amenât les ambassadeurs romains, et il les reçut avec l'affabilité dont Attila était capable.

'Pour cette entrevue solennelle, les négociateurs avaient pris les insignes de leur plus haute dignité; l'histoire nous dit que Léon s'était revêtu de ses habits pontificaux, et une révélation de la tombe nous a fait reconnaître en quoi ce vêtement consistait.[1] Léon portait une mitre de soie brochée d'or, arrondie à la manière orientale, une chasuble de pourpre brune, avec un pallium orné d'une petite croix rouge sur l'épaule droite, et d'une autre plus

[1] Erat indutus pontificalibus indumentis . . . super humero dextro crux parvà rubri coloris. . . . Telle est la description des vêtements pontificaux avec lesquels saint Léon fut enseveli et qu'on trouva dans sa tombe lors de la translation de ses reliques. On en peut voir tout le détail dans les Bollandistes à la date du 11 avril. Nous devons à ce procès-verbal de translation d'avoir pu décrire le costume que portait saint Léon à l'audience d'Attila, puisque c'étaient là ses habits pontificaux, et que son biographe nous dit qu'il aborda le roi des Huns en costume pontifical, *augustiore habitu.*

grande au côté gauche de la poitrine. Sitôt qu'il parut, il devint l'objet de l'attention et des prévenances du roi des Huns. Ce fut lui qui exposa les propositions de l'empereur, du sénat, et du peuple romain. En quels termes le fit-il ? Comment parvint-il à déguiser sous la dignité du langage ce qu'avait de honteux une demande de paix sans combat ? comment conserva-t-il encore à sa ville quelque grandeur en la montrant à genoux ? Par quelle inspiration merveilleuse sut-il contenir dans les bornes du respect ce barbare enflé d'orgueil, qui faisait payer si cher sa clémence par la moquerie et le dédain ? S'il invoqua la puissance des saints apôtres pour protéger la cité gardienne de leurs tombeaux, s'il rappela le conquérant aux sentiments de sa propre fragilité par l'exemple de la fragilité des nations, nous ne pouvons que le supposer : l'histoire qui nous voile si souvent ses secrets, a voulu nous dérober celui-là. Un chroniqueur contemporain, Prosper d'Aquitaine, qui fut secrétaire de Léon, ou du moins son collaborateur dans plusieurs ouvrages, nous dit seulement "qu'il s'en remit à l'assistance de Dieu, que ne fait jamais défaut aux efforts des justes, et que le succès couronna sa foi." Attila lui accorda ce qu'il était venut chercher, la paix moyennant un tribut annuel, et promit de quitter l'Italie. L'accord fut conclu le 6 juillet, jour de l'octave des apôtres saint Pierre et saint Paul.'

The position of the Christian hierarchy after the invasions is thus pointedly described by M. Guizot, *Hist. de la Civilisation en France*, viiime leçon :—

'Quand les barbares se furent établis, voici dans quelle situation se trouve l'église, au moins ce qu'elle devint bientôt. Les évêques étaient, vous le savez, les chefs naturels des villes : ils administraient le peuple dans l'intérieur de chaque cité ; ils le représentaient auprès des barbares ; ils étaient ses magistrats au-dedans ses protecteurs au-dehors. Le clergé avait donc dans le régime municipal, c'est-à-dire, dans ce qui restait de la société romaine, de profondes racines. Il en poussa bientôt ailleurs ; les évêques de-vinrent les conseillers des rois barbares. Ils les conseillèrent sur la conduite qu'ils avaient à tenir avec les peuples vaincus, sur ce qu'ils devaient faire pour devenir les héritiers des empereurs romains. Ils avaient beaucoup plus d'expérience et d'intelligence politique que les barbares à peine sortis de Germanie ; ils avaient le goût de pouvoir ; ils étaient accoutumés à le servir et à en profiter. Ils furent donc les conseillers de la royauté naissante, en restant les magistrats et les patrons de la municipalité encore debout.

'Les voilà établis, d'une part auprès du people, de l'autre auprès des trônes. Ce n'est pas tout ; une troisième situation commence bientôt pour eux ; ils deviennent de grands propriétaires ; ils entrent dans cette organisation hiérarchique de la propriété foncière, qui n'existait pas encore, mais tendait à se former ; ils travaillent et réussissent très-promptement à y occuper une grande place. En sorte qu'à cette époque, dans les premiers rudiments de la société nouvelle, déjà l'église tient à tout, est partout accréditée et puissante ; symptôme assuré qu'elle atteindra la première à la domination. Ce fut, en effet, ce qui arriva.'

NOTE L. Page 124.

Tertullian, at the beginning of the third century, seems to be the first of the Christians who remarked in the hostile attitude of the Northern barbarians the vengeance which might possibly yet be wreaked upon the persecutors of his faith. *Apol. Adv. Gent.* c. 37 :—'Si enim et hostes exsertos, non tantum vindices occultos agere vellemus, deesset nobis vis numerorum et copiarum ? Plures nimirum Mauri et *Marcomanni*, ipsique Parthi, vel quantæcunque unius tamen loci et suorum finium gentes, quam totius orbis.'

In the next generation, during the seventh persecution, Commodianus, writing rude verses for the multitude, makes a very shrewd and particular prophecy on the subject :—

'Sed erit initium septima persecutio nostra.
Ecce, januam pulsat et jam cognoscitur ense,
Qui cito trajiciet Gothis irrumpentibus amnem.
Rex Apolyon erit cum ipsis, nomine dirus,
Qui persecutionem dissipet sanctorum ; in armis
Pergit ad Romam cum multa millia gentis,
Decretoque Dei captivat ex parte subactos.
Multi senatorum tunc enim captivi deflebunt,
Et Deum cœlorum blasphemant a barbaro victi.'

'In the eyes of the heathens,' says Krafft (*Anfänge*, &c., p. 3), 'the fearful onslaughts of the barbarians in the third century, in connection with repeatedly recurring plagues and famines, appeared as a chastisement of the gods, whose worship had fallen into decay in many parts of the empire through the diffusion of Christianity. In replying to the reproaches of the Pagans on this head, Cyprian (circa 253) recognises the barbarians on the frontier among the signs of coming evil which were only too apparent. Cyprian, *Ad Demetrianum.* See also the tract *De Mortalitate.* Compare Arnobius, *Adv. Gentes*, i. 4. 16.'

As the perils of the empire from the assaults of the barbarians became more apparent, while the Pagans referred all their calamities to the anger of their gods at the prevalence of the new faith, the Christians, not less shocked at the signs of the times, ascribed them to the corruption of the world, which as they expected would suddenly be dissolved.

'When upon the death of the victorious Theodosius the enemies of Rome arose again in arms, and no deliverer appeared, the thoughts of Chrysostom, overpowered as he was by the terrors of the crisis, reverted to the idea of a proximate end of the world. . . . . At one time he beheld, in wars, tribulations, and earthquakes, tokens of a world growing old and nearing its dissolution, and compares them with the innumerable sufferings with which the perishing body of man is afflicted, or with the signs that precede the fall of a house. He points to a specific period, the year

400 from Christ:—"Ita si tot annorum quadringentesimum esse finem dixerimus non aberrabimus." Again he sees in the calamities of the time, its famines, plagues, earthquakes, and wars, a punishment for the sins of mankind, and for their increasing corruption. . . . . The day of fulfilment delays yet a while: the Lord hath not designated it expressly to His apostles, in order that they might keep ever on the watch.[1] Notwithstanding this expectation of the approaching end, Chrysostom allows himself, as Patriarch of Constantinople, to persist in prosecuting the conversion of the Arian Goths to the Catholic creed, and the still heathen barbarians to Christianity. Yet even that was a sign of the end: the Gospel must be preached to all nations.[2] At the same time Jerome was raising his lament from the East over the calamities of the day.

'Not long after the death of Theodosius, in the year 396, he writes to Heliodorus, Bishop of Altinum[3]:—"For twenty years and more (since 375) Roman blood has flowed daily between Constantinople and the Julian Alps. Scythia, Thrace, Macedonia, Dardania, Dacia, Thessalonica, Achaia, Epirus, Dalmatia, and all Pannonia are devastated by the fury of the Goths, the Sarmatians, the Quadi, Alani, the Huns, the Vandals, and the Marcomanni. How many matrons, how many holy virgins, have been made the sport of these monsters! Bishops have been captured, priests and other clergy slain, churches overthrown, horses stalled at the altars of Christ, and the remains of martyrs rooted up. Everywhere sorrow and sighing and death meet the eye. The Roman Empire is falling to pieces, and yet our stiff necks are not bowed:

> 'Non mihi, si linguæ centum sint, oraque centum,
> Ferrea vox, ...
> Omnia pœnarum percurrere nomina possim.'

[1] Homil. xxxiv. on *Joh.* iv. 28 ff.; Homil. on 2 *Tim.* iii. 1; Homil. on *Matth.* vi. 16; Homil. vii. on *Ephesians.*

[2] Homil. on *Matth.* vi. 16.

[3] *Epist.* 25. Comp. Epist. ad Ageruchiam.

Long have we suffered God's wrath, and yet appease Him not. Through our sins the barbarians are strong; for our crimes the Roman arms are overcome." . . . .

'In conclusion, Jerome would wish to cast a glance over the world as from a watch-tower:—"Then would I show you the ruin of the whole globe—people at war with people, kingdom with kingdom, some tortured, others slain, some swept away by the waves, others carried into captivity . . . . in short, the destruction of the race of men now existing upon all the face of the earth."

'S. Jerome was occupied at the moment with the exposition of Ezekiel, when the news of the devastation of Italy by Alaric and the Goths, the siege laid to Rome, and the death of many of his friends, was reported to him. Day and night did he ponder on the fate of his Christian brethren, and hovered between hope and fear. When at last he learnt the fate of Rome, "That the shining light of the world was extinguished, and the head of the Roman Empire fallen"—"et ut verius dicam in una urbe totus orbus interiit,"—then was he struck dumb in his anguish, and laid by his work. Once he writes to Marcellinus: he knew not, as the proverb says, his own words, and kept silence, well knowing that it was the time for tears.[1] . . . .

'In the West the same sorrowful apprehensions arose of the approaching end of the world, as the dangers which menaced the Roman Empire from the barbarians drew nigher and nigher. S. Ambrose imagined that in the Goths who threatened Italy he beheld the terrible Gog and Magog of the last day, foretold by Ezekiel and in the Apocalypse—a conclusion to which the very name of the Goths may have helped to lead him.'[2] . . . —Krafft, *Anfänge*, p. 25, foll.

[1] *Præfat.* in Ezech.; *Epist.* 78, ad Marcellinum et Anapsychiam.

[2] *De Fide, Ad Gratianum*, lib. ii. 16 (A.D. 378, 379). So Jerome, *Liber Quæstion. Hebr.*, *In Genes.* (on Genes. x.): 'Scio quendam Gog et Magog tam de præsenti loco

Note M. Page 126.

After describing the siege and sack of Rome by Alaric and the Goths, Zeller (*Antiquité et Moyen Age*, p. 227, foll.) proceeds to remark:—

'Ce qui est plus curieux à connaître que les détails de ce pillage de la ville éternelle, c'est l'effet que cet événement produisit dans l'univers romain. Les derniers païens en furent atterrés; l'immobile rocher du Capitole avait tremblé; Virgile avait dit en vain:

"His ego nec metas rerum nec tempora pono."

'Les oracles du paganisme et ses poëtes étaient convaincus de mensonge. C'etaient les chrétiens qui avaient bien vu et véridiquement prédit. Un cri de joie s'échappe presque de leur bouche. "Depuis longtemps," dit saint Augustin, dans une lettre à Victorianus, "l'évangile et les prophètes avaient prédit toutes ces choses. Il ne nous convient pas de vous mettre en contradiction avec nous-mêmes, de croire aux prophéties que nous lisons et de nous plaindre de leur accomplissement. Ce sont plutôt ceux que sont incrédules à l'égard des saints livres qui doivent ajouter foi à leur vérité, maintenant que les paroles sacrées s'accomplissent." Un Romain accuse Augustin de se réjouir de cette funeste nouvelle. "Mon cœur affligé," répond-il, "et ma conscience de chré-

quam de Jezechiel *ad Gothorum* nuper in terra nostra bacchantium *historiam* retulisse: quod utrum verum sit, prælii ipsius fine monstratur. Et certe Gothos omnes retro eruditi *magis Getas* quam Gog et Magog appellare consueverunt.' But he reverts again to this derivation. Præf. ix. lib. xi. *In Ezechiel.* Comp. S. Ambrose, *Exposit. Evang. sec. Luc.* lib. q. 'Verborum autem cœlestium nulli magis, quam nos, testes sumus, quos mundi finis invenit. . . . . ergo quia in occasu sæculi sumus præcedunt quædam ægritudines mundi. Ægritudo mundi est fames, ægritudo mundi est pestilentia, ægritudo mundi est persecutio.' See also *Serm. de Bellico Tumultu.*

Again: *Expos. Evan. sec. Luc.* l. c. 'Prædicetur Evangelium et sæculum destruatur.' Sicut enim præcessit in orbem terræ evangelii prædicatio, cui jam et Gothi et Armenii crediderunt, et ideo mundi finem videmus,' etc.

tien protestent;" mais Paul Orose, son disciple, dans son Histoire Ecclésiastique, ne dissimule point ses vrais sentiments. "Pour qu'on ne doute point," dit-il, "que ces événements se sont accomplis pour châtier la corruption et les blasphèmes de Rome, la foudre du ciel est tombée, pour les achever, sur les monuments romains qu'avaient épargnés les barbares."'

See also p. 205, foll. :—

'On a accusé l'église chrétienne d'avoir manqué de patriotisme à la veille de ce grand cataclysme, d'avoir désespéré de l'empire et presque appelé de ses vœux les barbares. On trouve, en effet, dans les écrivains chrétiens, plus d'un passage qui témoigne de cette espèce de découragement et d'une sorte d'espérance vague mêlée cependant de crainte en face de l'invasion. Mais il n'y avait plus réellement de patriotisme dans l'empire; il avait disparu avec le vieux culte romain. Quand un nouveau malheur arrivait, combien de païens, avec l'historien Zosime, dénonçaient l'abandon de la vieille religion, et le mépris des dieux comme la cause de tout le mal! Le sage Ammien-Marcellin seul voit autour de lui trop de causes naturelles de ce qui arrive, sans en chercher encore de surnaturelles. Quand il nous raconte ces échecs répétés des légions devant les barbares ou la fin misérable d'un empereur romain brûlé par eux dans une chaumière, il laisse bien percer de temps en temps la colère du vaincu; mais sa douleur ne l'empêche pas de reconnaître que la faute en était toute aux Romains, aux officiers, et aux soldats. Zosime lui-même ne nous avoue-t-il pas que, dans certaines provinces, les citoyens, opprimés par les exacteurs, regardaient la conquête du pays par les barbares comme un événement heureux, et se résignaient à une invasion qui devait les délivrer du malheur de posséder?

'En réalité, le vieux sentiment national de Rome s'était éteint dans une sorte de cosmopolitisme sans grandeur, et l'église sentait qu'elle ne pouvait attacher ses destinées au colosse qui s'écroulait. Saint Augustin écrit au milieu des ruines son livre de la *Cité de*

Dieu, société choisie qui accomplit son pèlerinage à travers les misères de cette vie pour mériter la cité céleste, la sainte Jérusalem qu'il rêve au-delà de la mort. Si Lactance s'écrie, "Comment ne pas craindre que la société ne croule pas avec Rome et que le monde ne périsse dans une seule ville ?" le nombre des chrétiens qui, pénétrés de la lecture de l'Écriture sainte, regardent l'invasion comme un châtiment providentiel des crimes des païens, est encore bien plus considérable. Saint Jérôme, en commentant Ézéchiel, applique à la ville de Rome les prophéties faites contre l'antique Babylone. On ne redoute l'invasion, dit saint Augustin, que de crainte d'être arraché à ses vices. Salvien, dans son curieux livre du *Gouvernement de Dieu*, n'hésite point, quand il compare les barbares aux Romains, à déclarer ses préférences: "Vous pensez," dit-il aux Romains, "être meilleurs que les barbares; ils sont hérétiques, païens, dites-vous, et vous êtes orthodoxes. . . . . Je réponds que par la foi nous sommes meilleurs, mais, par notre vie, je dis avec larmes que nous somme pires. Vous connaissez la loi et vous la voilez; ils sont hérétiques et ne le savent pas. . . . . Et nous nous étonnons que Dieu livre nos provinces aux barbares quand leur pudeur purifie la terre encore toute souillée des débauches romaines." Tandis que les bandes de Bagaudes, formées de colons révoltés et de citoyens fuyant devant le fisc, donnent la main aux barbares, les chrétiens les appellent.

'"Les barbares viennent," dit Salvien aux Romains, "et vos désordres, vos crimes, vous ont tellement abrutis que vous ne craignez même pas le danger où vous êtes; vous ne voulez point périr et vous ne cherchez point votre salut; les barbares sont là et vous ne songez qu'à manger, à boire, à dormir. Dieu a répandu sur vous ce léthargique assoupissement qui est la prélude de la mort. Je voudrais faire entendre au monde entier ces paroles: Romains, ayez honte de tous vos vices; les barbares sont plus forts que vous, parce qu'ils sont moins vicieux; votre faiblesse, elle est dans vos âmes; vous êtes vaincus par vos vices. Venez, Goths,

Huns et Saxons; nous avons des chrétiens, ils lisent l'Évangile, mais ils font la débauche; ils écoutent les apôtres, mais ils s'enivrent; ils suivent le Christ, mais ils sont des voleurs."

'On ne peut pas dire cependant que l'Église ait trahi l'Empire Romain. Elle ne déserte pas; elle passe par-dessus les Romains et les barbares et ne voit en eux que des hommes à convertir. Saint Augustin proteste, dans plus d'un endroit, contre la lâcheté que montreraient les prêtres s'ils abandonnaient leur poste devant les malheurs publics. "Ceux," dit-il, "qui prennent la fuite ou qui ne restent que par la force, s'ils viennent à être pris, souffrent pour eux-mêmes et non pour leurs frères; la crainte des maux ne doit pas nous faire abandonner notre ministère." Et il devait plus tard lui-même, Hippone assiégée par les Vandales, confirmer ces paroles par sa belle mort.

'On ne peut trouver étonnant que le christianisme n'ait point confondu ses destinées avec celles de la société romaine. Il avait conquis l'État sans doute, et depuis les empereurs jusqu'aux esclaves, il dominait toute la société. Mais combien d'empereurs, à commencer par Constantin, ne l'avaient pris pour un instrument politique! Que de fils de nobles ou de riches familles n'avaient vu dans la foi nouvelle qu'un moyen de parvenir; puis, selon les circonstances, étaient retournés au vieux culte! Les apostasies de ce genre étaient si nombreuses que les empereurs se croyaient obligés de les punir de la perte des droits civils. Les livres des Pères sont pleins de lamentations sur ces mauvais chrétiens, ces faux convertis qui introduisent dans l'Église leurs superstitions, leur indifférence ou leur impiété, sur ce peuple incorrigible que le retard de la flotte de l'Égypte, chargée du grain des distributions, suffit pour ramener aux sacrifices de Neptune, et qui, à l'époque des Lupercales, parcourt nu les rues de la ville, frappant les femmes pour les rendre fécondes. Le mysticisme chrétien avait alors quelque chose de trop amollissant, la piété était trop détachée de la terre pour rendre au patriotisme romain les mâles vertus qui eussent pu sauver l'empire. Mais on conçoit que l'Église espérât mieux des superstitions barbares moins enracinées, et de mœurs plus grossières, mais moins corrompues. Elle se disposait, non à sauver l'empire, mais à dompter l'orgueil, la férocité des vainqueurs, à adoucir les misères des vaincus, et à préparer leur union dans la commune patrie du christianisme.'

If what has been advanced in my text (Lecture V.) and Note E, regarding the reciprocal action of Christianity and Paganism upon each other in the fourth and fifth centuries be founded in fact, the remarks of M. Guizot (*Histoire de la Civilisation en France*, six^{me} leçon) may be considered a little one-sided. 'C'est le moment où l'ancienne philosophie expire, où commence la théologie moderne; où l'une se transforme pour ainsi dire dans l'autre; où certaines systèmes deviennent des dogmes, certaines écoles des sectes. Ces époques de transition sont d'une grande importance, et peut-être, sous le point de vue historique, les plus instructives de toutes.' True: but a great part of the instruction to be derived from such history regards the influence exerted even in the decline and disappearance of the older forms of thought upon the newer; an influence strongly marked, as I conceive, in the approximation of Christian ideas to the Pagan at the period under review.

But looking at the question from M. Guizot's point of view, some of his remarks are extremely interesting.

'C'est surtout dans le midi de la Gaule que ce caractère du vme siècle se manifeste avec évidence. Vous avez vu quelle activité y régnait dans la société religieuse, entre autres dans les monastères de Lerins et de S. Victor, foyer de tant d'opinions hardies. Tout ce mouvement d'esprit ne venait pas du christianisme: c'était dans les mêmes contrées . . . . que l'ancienne civilisation sur son déclin s'était pour ainsi dire concentrée et conservait encore le plus de vie. . . . . Tout atteste, en un mot, que, sous le point de vue philosophique comme sous le point de vue religieux, la Gaule romaine et grecque, aussi bien que chrétienne, était, à cette époque, en Occident du moins, la portion la plus animée, la plus vivante de l'empire. Aussi est-ce là que la transition de la philosophie païenne à la théologie chrétienne, du monde ancien au monde moderne, est le plus clairement empreinte, et se laisse le mieux observer. . . . .

'Ainsi éclate le fait que j'ai indiqué en commençant, la fusion de la philosophie païenne et de la théologie chrétienne, la métamorphose de l'une dans l'autre. Et il y a ceci de remarquable, que l'argumentation destinée à établir la spiritualité de l'âme vient évidemment de l'ancienne philosophie plus que du christianisme, et que l'auteur (Mamert Claudien) semble surtout s'appliquer à convaincre les théologiens en leur prouvant que la foi chrétienne n'a rien en ceci qui ne se concilie à merveille avec les résultats auxquels conduit la raison. . . . . Ce que l'ancienne philosophie conservait de force et de vie passait au service des chrétiens; c'était sous la forme religieuse, et au sein même du christianisme, que se reproduisaient les idées, les écoles, toute la science des philosophes. . . . .

'C'est là le mouvement que vinrent arrêter l'invasion des Barbares et la chute de l'Empire Romain: cent ans plus tard, on ne trouve plus aucune trace de ce que je viens de mettre sous vos yeux, ... toute cette activité intellectuelle de la Gaule, au viime siècle, il n'en est plus question.

'La perte fut-elle grande? l'invasion des Barbares étouffa-t-elle un mouvement important et fécond? J'en doute fort. Rappelez-vous ce que j'ai l'honneur de vous dire sur le caractère essentiellement pratique du christianisme; le progrès intellectuel, la science proprement dite, n'était point son but; et bien qu'il se rattachât sur plusieurs points à l'ancienne philosophie, bien qu'il sût s'approprier ses idées et en tirer bon parti, il ne s'inquiétait guère de la continuer, ni de la remplacer: changer les mœurs, gouverner la vie, telle était la pensée dominante de ses chefs. . . . .

'Ce que l'invasion des Barbares et la chute de l'Empire Romain arrêtèrent surtout, détruisirent même, ce fut le mouvement intellectuel; ce qui restait de science, de philosophie, de liberté d'esprit au vme siècle, disparut sous leurs coups. Mais le mouvement moral, la réforme pratique du christianisme, et l'établissement officiel de son autorité sur les peuples, n'en furent point frappés; peut-être même y gagnèrent-ils au lieu de perdre. . . . .

'L'invasion des Barbares ne tua donc point ce qui avait vie; au fond, l'activité et la liberté intellectuelles étaient en décadence; tout porte à croire qu'elles se seraient arrêtées d'elles-mêmes; les Barbares les arrêtèrent plus durement et plus tôt. C'est là, je crois, tout ce qu'on peut leur imputer.'

Note N. Page 143.

The translation given in the text was made from memory, but it is sufficiently near to the purport of the well-known passage in Bede's History, the speech of Coifi on the preaching of S. Paulinus before the King of Northumbria (*Hist. Eccl.* ii. 13):—

'Talis mihi videtur, rex, vita hominum præsens in terris ad comparationem ejus quod nobis incertum est temporis, quale cum te residente ad cœnam cum ministris tuis tempore brumali, accenso quidem foco in medio et calido effecto cœnaculo, furentibus autem foris per omnia turbinibus hiemalium pluviarum vel nivium, adveniensque unus passerum domum citissimè pervolaverit; qui cum per unum ostium ingrediens mox per aliud exierit. Ipso quidem tempore quo intus est hiemis tempestate non tangitur, sed tamen parvissimo spatio serenitatis ad momentum excurso, mox de hieme in hiemem regrediens tuis oculis elabitur. Ita hæc vita hominum ad modicum apparet; quid autem sequatur, quidve præcesserit, prorsus ignoramus. Unde si hæc nova doctrina certius aliquid attulit, merito esse sequenda videtur.'

Note O. Page 163.

In Menzel's *Geschichte der Deutschen*, there is a special chapter on the 'Respect paid to Women' among the ancient Germans. (Book i. chap. 19.)

'Im heidnischen Alterthume wurden die Frauen meist verachtet und als niedere Wesen angesehen. Bei den Deutschen aber standen sie schon in den ältesten Zeiten an Ehre den Männern gleich, ja sie wurden in mancher Beziehung sogar als höhere Wesen angesehen. Man glaubte, sagt Tacitus, es sey etwas Heiliges und Prophetisches in ihnen (inesse quia etiam sanctum aliquid et providum putant). Die Frauenehre übte auf Sitten und Gemüth der Deutschen, und dadurch auch auf ihre Kunst und Poesie, einen solchen Einfluss, dass hierin vorzüglich die Quelle des sogenannten Romantischen zu suchen ist, dass die Eigenthümlichkeit der neueren Kunst und Sitte im Gegensatz gegen die orientalische und griechisch-römische oder antike geworden ist.

'Die alten Deutschen erkannten, dass dieses Heilige in den Frauen von der höchsten Reinheit abhinge. Daher war in ihren Sitten und Gesetzen die Wahrung nicht nur der äussern Ehre, sondern auch der innern Unschuld des weiblichen Geschlechts eine der festesten Grundregeln. Schon Tacitus rühmt diese unverbrüchliche Sittenstrenge und Heiligachtung der Keuschheit, und sagt, so viel er an den Germanen loben müsse, sey doch diese Sittlichkeit, als die Grundlage aller andern Volkstugenden, am meisten zu loben (nec ullam morum partem magis laudaveris).

'Die Mädchen wurden in Unschuld aufgezogen, unter häuslichen Arbeiten, fern von den wilden Gelagen der Männer, ausser wenn sie im elterlichen Hause Gäste bedienten. Sie kamen erst spät in die Ehe. Ihre kräftigere Natur entwickelte sich langsamer. Noch jetzt werden die Nordländer, und besonders die noch den alten Sitten treuer gebliebenen Gebirgsvölker, später mannbar als die üppigeren Südländer und Städtebewohner. . . . .

'Verbrechen gegen die weibliche Zucht und Ehre wurden als unversöhnlich angesehen und behandelt. Der jungfräuliche Ehrenkranz, den die Braut bei der Hochzeit trug, ist wahrscheinlich eine uralte Sitte bei den Deutschen. Keine durfte ihn tragen, auf deren Ehre der geringste Makel haftete. Eine erwiesene Verleumdung in dieser Beziehung wurde mit ungewöhnlicher Härte bestraft. Gewalt an Jungfrauen wurde unter allen Umständen mit entehrendem Tode bestraft, und noch ziemlich spät im Mittelalter ist in den im Schwabenspiegel gesammelten Gesetzen die Verordnung enthalten, in einem Hause, wo ein solcher Frevel geschehen, alles bis auf das Vieh umbringen und das Haus selbst der Erde gleich zu machen. . . . .

'Eine der schönsten und weisesten Sitten war die, dass man den Töchtern keine Mitgift gab. Sie wurden daher nicht um des Vermögens, sondern nur der Tugend und Schönheit willen begehrt und zur Ehe genommen. Erst in der späten christlichen Zeit kamen die Ausstattungen auf. Zur Zeit des Tacitus brachte die Jungfrau ihrem Bräutigam nur einige Waffen mit, zur Erinnerung, dass er sie für sie führen solle. Dagegen musste der Bräutigam dem Vater, Bruder, oder sonstigem Vormund der Braut die Vormundschaft oder das Recht, sie vor Gericht zu vertreten, um eine herkömmliche Summe abkaufen. Die Verlobten wechselten Handschlag, Kuss und Ring. In der heidnischen Zeit herrschte der Gebrauch, drei Nächte lang zwischen Neuvermählte ein blankes und scharfes Schwert zu legen, auf einem religiösen Aberglauben. Die Hochzeit wurde, wie schon ihr Name zeigt, als hohe Zeit, als der Höhepunkt im Leben, so öffentlich als möglich und mit grossem Jubel vieler Gäste gefeiert. Nach der Hochzeit gab der junge Ehemann der jungen Frau ein Geschenk, die Morgengabe genannt, das ihr eigen blieb bis an den Tod, und das Niemand wiedernehmen oder abstreiten durfte, wenn sie nur mit der Hand auf der Brust beschwor, es sey ihre Morgengabe. . . . .

'Der Ehebruch war so unversöhnlich wie die Beleidigung der

Jungfrauen. Wollte der Mann die ehebrecherische Frau nicht selber sogleich tödten, so wurde sie nackt mit geschornem Haupt aus dem Hause gestossen und von den Nachbarinnen fortgepeitscht von Ortschaft zu Ortschaft, bis sie liegen blieb. Schon Tacitus lobt diese Sitte, die auch noch viel später bei den Sachsen sich erheilt. . . . . Die alten Deutschen hielten die Schonung der sogenannten Herzensschwächen nicht für so dringend, um darüber die öffentlichen Sitten erschlaffen und ein ganzes Volk liederlich werden zu lassen. Als sie mit den Römern näher bekannt wurden, und man ihnen beständig sagte, ihre Keuschheit war barbarisch, sie seyen viel zu streng, da nahm das burgundische Gesetz auf diese Vorwürfe Rücksicht, und fügte die Verordnung, dass Ehebruch nach wie vor unnachsichtlich mit dem Tode gestraft werden solle, die denkwürdigen Worte hinzu: "Denn es ist gerechter, dass Alle durch die Verurtheilung weniger gebessert werden, als dass unter dem Vorwand, die alte Barbarei zu verdrängen, nur Gelegenheit zu Lastern gegeben werde." Darum rühmte man auch von den Gothen und Vandalen, dass sie nicht nur selbst keusch geblieben sind, sondern sogar auch die verdorbenen Römer wieder keusch gemacht hätten.

'Die altdeutschen Frauen wurden so geachtet, dass man sie im Wergeld höher schätzte als die Männer, bei Allemannen und Bayern noch einmal, bei Franken und Thüringern dreimal so hoch, und noch höher wenn sie guter Hoffnung waren. . . . . Alle Frauen durften Waffen führen, wenn sie sie zu brauchen verstanden. Ihre Stimme wurde im Rath der Männer gehört. Kluge Frauen standen nicht selten an der Spitze grosser Unternehmungen.' . . . .

The chivalrous feelings of respect towards women, which form so marked an element in Teutonic life in the middle ages, are traced by the antiquarians to the notion, common among the primitive German races, of a close intercourse between the flower of their heroes and the superior female existences, to whom they gave the name of Walkyren.

'Walkyren waren die himmlischen Mädchen, von denen die uralten Deutschen glaubten, dass sie jede Schlacht umschwebten, die Helden auswählten, welche fallen sollten, und dann mit ihnen in Walhalla als ihren ewigen Geliebten himmlische Freuden genössen. Daher war dem Helden jeder Tod auf dem Schlachtfeld ein Brautfest für den Himmel. Aber auch irdische Jungfrauen dachte man sich als Walkyren, wenn sie die Rüstung anlegten und Schildjungfrauen wurden. Das zarte poetische Verhältniss des heidnischen Helden zu seiner himmlischen Geliebten ging später in das Verhältniss des christlichen Helden zu seiner Dame über, und diese war nicht immer eine irdische Dame, sondern die heilige Jungfrau oder eine andere Heilige. Die romantische Liebe des Mittelalters, der schwärmerische Ritterdienst, der göttlichen Wesen, oder unbekannten, oder stolzen und ewig undankbaren Damen gewidmet war, und das, was man im edeln Sinne den Minnedienst und die Galanterie nannte, hatte seinen ersten Ursprung aus dem schönen heidnischen Glauben an die Walkyren.' (Menzel, *Geschichte der Deutschen*, book i. chap. 20.)

THE END.

LIST OF WORKS

PUBLISHED BY D. APPLETON & CO.,

Nos. 443 & 445 Broadway, N. Y.

A Descriptive Catalogue, with full titles and prices, may be had gratuitously on application.

About's Roman Question.
Adams' Boys at Home.
—— Edgar Clifton.
Addison's Spectator. 6 vols.
Adler's German and English Dictionary.
—— Abridged do. do. do.
—— German Reader.
—— " Literature.
—— Ollendorff for Learning German.
—— Key to the Exercises.
—— Iphigenia in Tauris.
After Icebergs with a Painter.
Agnel's Book of Chess.
Aguilar's Home Influence.
—— Mother's Recompense.
—— Days of Bruce. 2 vols.
—— Home Scenes.
—— Woman's Friendship.
—— Women of Israel. 2 vols.
—— Vale of Cedars.
Ahn's French Method.
—— Spanish Grammar.
—— A Key to same.
—— German Method. 1 vol.
Or, separately—First Course. 1 vol.
Second " 1 vol.
Aids to Faith. A series of Essays, by Various Writers.
Aikin's British Poets. From Chaucer to the Present Time. 3 vols.
Album for Postage Stamps.
Albums of Foreign Galleries; in 7 folios.
Alden's Elements of Intellectual Philosophy.
Alison's Miscellaneous Essays.
Allen's Mechanics of Nature.
Alsop's Charms of Fancy.
Amelia's Poems.
American Poets (Gems from the).
American Eloquence. A Collection of Speeches and Addresses. 2 vols.
American System of Education:
1. Hand-Book of Anglo-Saxon Root-Words.
2. Hand-Book of Anglo-Saxon Derivatives.
American System of Education:
3. Hand-Book of Engrafted Words.
Anderson's Mercantile Correspondence.
Andrews' New French Instructor.
—— A Key to the above.
Annals of San Francisco.
Antisell on Coal Oils.
Anthon's Law Student.
Appletons' New American Cyclopædia of Useful Knowledge. 16 vols.
—— Annual Cyclopædia, and Register of Important Events for 1861, '62, '63, '64, '65.
—— Cyclopædia of Biography, Foreign and American.
—— Cyclopædia of Drawing.
The same in parts:
Topographical Drawing.
Perspective and Geometrical Drawing.
Shading and Shadows.
Drawing Instruments and their Uses.
Architectural Drawing and Design.
Mechanical Drawing and Design.
—— Dictionary of Mechanics and Engineering. 2 large vols.
—— Railway Guide.
—— American Illustrated Guide Book. 1 vol.
Do. do., separately:
1. Eastern and Middle States, and British Provinces. 1 vol.
2. Southern and Western States, and the Territories. 1 vol.
—— Companion Hand-Book of Travel.
Arabian Nights' Entertainments.
Arnold's (S. G.) History of the State of Rhode Island. 2 vols.
Arnold's (Dr.) History of Rome.
—— Modern History.
Arnold's Classical Series:
—— First Latin Book.
—— First and Second Latin Book and Grammar.
—— Latin Prose Composition.
—— Cornelius Nepos.
—— First Greek Book.
—— Greek Prose Composition Book, 1.

Arnold's Greek Prose Composition Book, 2.
—— Greek Reading Book.
Arthur's (T. S.) Tired of Housekeeping.
Arthur's (W.) Successful Merchant.
At Anchor; or, A Story of our Civil War.
Atlantic Library. 7 vols. in case.
Attaché in Madrid.
Aunt Fanny's Story Book.
—— Mitten Series. 6 vols. in case.
—— Night Cap Series. 6 vols. in case.

Badois' English Grammar for Frenchmen.
—— A Key to the above.
Baine's Manual of Composition and Rhetoric.
Bakewell's Great Facts
Baldwin's Flush Times.
—— Party Leaders.
Balmanno's Pen and Pencil.
Bank Law of the United States.
Barrett's Beauty for Ashes.
Bartlett's U. S. Explorations. 2 vols.
—— Cheap edition. 2 vols. in 1.
Barwell's Good in Every Thing.
Bassnett's Theory of Storms.
Baxley's West Coast of America and Hawaiian Islands.
Beach's Pelayo. An Epic.
Beall (John Y.), Trial of.
Beauties of Sacred Literature.
Beauties of Sacred Poetry.
Beaumont and Fletcher's Works. 2 vols.
Belem's Spanish Phrase Book.
Bello's Spanish Grammar (in Spanish).
Benedict's Run Through Europe.
Benton on the Dred Scott Case.
—— Thirty Years' View. 2 vols.
—— Debates of Congress. 16 vols.
Bertha Percy. By Margaret Field. 12mo.
Bertram's Harvest of the Sea. Economic and Natural History of Fishes.
Bessie and Jessie's Second Book.
Beza's Novum Testamentum.
Bibles in all styles of bindings and various prices.
Bible Stories, in Bible Language.
Black's General Atlas of the World.
Bloomfield's Farmer's Boy.
Blot's What to Eat, and How to Cook it.
Blue and Gold Poets. 6 vols. in case.
Boise's Greek Exercises.
—— First Three Books of Xenophon's Anabasis.
Bojesen's Greek and Roman Antiquities.
Book of Common Prayer. Various prices.
Boone's Life and Adventures.
Bourne's Catechism of the Steam Engine.
—— Hand-Book of the Steam Engine.
—— Treatise on the Steam Engine.
Boy's Book of Modern Travel.
—— Own Toy Maker
Bradford's Peter the Great.
Bradley's (Mary E.) Douglass Farm.
Bradley's (Chas.) Sermons.
Brady's Christmas Dream.
Breakfast, Dinner, and Tea.
British Poets. From Chaucer to the Present Time. 8 large vols.
British Poets. Cabinet Edition. 15 vols.
Brooks' Ballads and Translations.
Brown, Jones, and Robinson's Tour.
Bryan's English Grammar for Germans.
Bryant & Stratton's Commercial Law.
Bryant's Poems, Illustrated.
—— Poems. 2 vols.
—— Thirty Poems.
—— Poems. Blue and Gold.
—— Letters from Spain.
Buchanan's Administration.
Buckle's Civilization in England. 2 vols.
—— Essays.
Bunyan's Divine Emblems.
Burdett's Chances and Changes.
—— Never Too Late.
Burgess' Photograph Manual. 12mo.
Burnett (James R.) on the Thirty-nine Articles.
Burnett (Peter H.), The Path which led a Protestant Lawyer to the Catholic Church.
Burnouf's Gramatica Latina.
Burns' (Jabez) Cyclopædia of Sermons.
Burns' (Robert) Poems.
Burton's Cyclopædia of Wit and Humor. 2 vols.
Butler's Martin Van Buren.
Butler's (F.) Spanish Teacher.
Butler's (S.) Hudibras.
Butler's (T. B.) Guide to the Weather.
Butler's (Wm. Allen) Two Millions.
Byron Gallery. The Gallery of Byron Beauties.
—— Poetical Works.
—— Life and Letters.
—— Works. Illustrated.

Cœleb's Laws and Practice of Whist.
Cæsar's Commentaries.
Caird's Prairie Farming.
Calhoun's Works and Speeches. 6 vols.
Campbell's (Thos.) Gertrude of Wyoming.
—— Poems.
Campbell (Judge) on Shakespeare.
Canot, Life of Captain.
Carlyle's (Thomas) Essays.
Carreno's Manual of Politeness.

Carreno's Compendio del Manual de Urbanidad.
Casseday's Poetic Lacon.
Cavendish's Laws of Whist.
Cervantes' Don Quixote, in Spanish.
—— Don Quixote, in English.
César L'Histoire de Jules. par S. M. I. Napoleon III. Vol. I., with Maps and Portrait. (French.)
Cheap Edition, without Maps and Portrait.
Maps and Portrait, for cheap edition, in envelopes.
Champlin's English Grammar.
—— Greek Grammar.
Chase on the Constitution and Canons.
Chaucer's Poems.
Chevalier on Gold.
Children's Holidays.
Child's First History.
Choquet's French Composition.
—— French Conversation.
Cicero de Officiis.
Chittenden's Report of the Peace Convention.
—— Select Orations.
Clarke's (D. S.) Scripture Promises.
Clarke's (Mrs. Cowden) Iron Cousin.
Clark's (H. J.) Mind in Nature.
Cleaveland and Backus' Villas and Cottages.
Cleveland's (H. W. S.) Hints to Riflemen.
Cloud Crystals. A Snow Flake Album.
Cobb's (J. B.) Miscellanies.
Coe's Spanish Drawing Cards. 10 parts.
Coe's Drawing Cards. 10 parts.
Colenso on the Pentateuch. 2 vols.
——— On the Romans.
Coleridge's Poems.
Collins' Amoor.
Collins' (T. W.) Humanics.
Collet's Dramatic French Reader.
Comings' Physiology.
——— Companion to Physiology.
Comment on Parle a Paris.
Congreve's Comedy.
Continental Library. 6 vols. in case.
Cooke's Life of Stonewall Jackson.
Cookery, by an American Lady.
Cooley's Cyclopædia of Receipts.
Cooper's Mount Vernon.
Copley's Early Friendship.
——— Poplar Grove.
Cornell's First Steps in Geography.
—— Primary Geography.
—— Intermediate Geography.
—— Grammar School Geography.
—— High School Geography and Atlas.
—— High School Geography.
—— " " Atlas.
—— Map Drawing. 12 maps in case.
—— Outline Maps, with Key. 13 maps in portfolio.
——— Or, the Key, separately.
Cornwall on Music.
Correlation and Conservation of Forces.
Cortez' Life and Adventures.
Cotter on the Mass and Rubrics.
Cottin's Elizabeth; or, the Exiles of Siberia.
Cousin Alice's Juveniles.
Cousin Carrie's Sun Rays.
——— Keep a Good Heart.
Cousin's Modern Philosophy. 2 vols.
——— On the True and Beautiful.
——— Only Romance.
Coutan's French Poetry.
Covell's English Grammar.
Cowles' Exchange Tables.
Cowper's Homer's Iliad.
——— Poems.
Cox's Eight Years in Congress, from 1857 to 1865.
Coxe's Christian Ballads.
Creasy on the English Constitution.
Crisis (The).
Crosby's (A.) Geometry.
Crosby's (H.) Œdipus Tyrannus.
Crosby's (W. H.) Quintus Curtius Rufus.
Crowe's Linny Lockwood.
Curry's Volunteer Book.
Cust's Invalid's Book.
Cyclopædia of Commercial and Business Anecdotes. 2 vols.

D'Abrantes' Memoires of Napoleon. 2 vols.
Dairyman's (The) Daughter.
Dana's Household Poetry.
Darwin's Origin of Species.
Dante's Poems.
Dasent's Popular Tales from the Norse.
Davenport's Christian Unity and its Recovery.
Dawson's Archaia.
De Belem's Spanish Phrase-Book.
De Fivas' Elementary French Reader.
—— Classic French Reader.
De Foe's Robinson Crusoe.
De Girardin's Marguerite.
——— Stories of an Old Maid.
De Hart on Courts Martial.
De L'Ardeche's History of Napoleon.
De Peyrac's Comment on Parle.
De Staël's Corinne, ou L'Italie.
De Veitelle's Mercantile Dictionary.
De Vere's Spanish Grammar.
Dew's Historical Digest.
Dickens's (Charles) Works. Original Illustrations. 24 vols.
Dies Irae and Stabat Mater, bound together.
Dies Irae, alone, and Stabat Mater, alone.
Dix's (John A.) Winter in Madeira.
—— Speeches and Addresses. 2 vols.

Dix's (Rev. M.) Lost Unity of the Christian World.
Dr. Oldham at Greystones, and his Talk there.
Doane's Works. 4 vols.
Downing's Rural Architecture.
Dryden's Poems.
Dunlap's Spirit History of Man.
Dusseldorf Gallery, Gems from the.
Dwight on the Study of Art.
Ebony Idol (The).
Ede's Management of Steel.
Edith Vaughan's Victory.
Egloffstein's Geology and Physical Geography of Mexico.
Eichhorn's German Grammar.
Elliot's Fine Work on Birds. 7 parts, or in 1 vol.
Ellsworth's Text-Book of Penmanship.
Ely's Journal.
Enfield's Indian Corn; its Value, Culture, and Uses.
Estvan's War Pictures.
Evans' History of the Shakers.
Evelyn's Life of Mrs. Godolphin.
Everett's Mount Vernon Papers.

Fables, Original and Selected.
Farrar's History of Free Thought.
Faustus.
Fay's Poems.
Fénélon's Telemaque.
——— The same, in 2 vols.
——— Telemachus.
Field's Bertha Percy.
Field's (M.) City Architecture.
Figuier's World before the Deluge.
Fireside Library. 8 vols. in case.
First Thoughts.
Fiji and the Fijians.
Flint's Physiology of Man.
Florian's William Tell.
Flower Pictures.
Fontana's Italian Grammar.
Foote's Africa and the American Flag.
Foresti's Italian Extracts.
Four Gospels (The).
Franklin's Man's Cry and God's Gracious Answer.
Frieze's Tenth and Twelfth Books of Quintilian.
Fullerton's (Lady G.) Too Strange Not to be True.
Funny Story Book.

Garland's Life of Randolph.
Gaskell's Life of Brontë. 2 vols.
The same, cheaper edition, in 1 vol.
George Ready.
Gerard's French Readings.
Gertrude's Philip Randolph.
Gesenius' Hebrew Grammar.
Ghostly Colloquies.

Gibbes' Documentary History. 3 vols.
Gibbons' Banks of New York.
Gilfillan's Literary Portraits.
Gillespie on Land Surveying.
Girardin on Dramatic Literature.
Goadby's Text-Book of Physiology.
Goethe's Iphigenia in Tauris.
Goldsmith's Essays.
——— Vicar of Wakefield.
Gosse's Evenings with the Microscope.
Goulburn's Office of the Holy Communion.
——— Idle Word.
——— Manual of Confirmation.
——— Sermons.
——— Study of the Holy Scriptures.
——— Thoughts on Personal Religion.
Gould's (E. S.) Comedy.
Gould's (W. M.) Zephyrs.
Graham's English Synonymes.
Grandmamma Easy's Toy Books.
Grandmother's Library. 6 vols. in case.
Grand's Spanish Arithmetic.
Grant's Report on the Armies of the United States 1864–'65.
Grauet's Portuguese Grammar.
Grayson's Theory of Christianity.
Greek Testament.
Greene's (F. H.) Primary Botany.
—— Class-Book of Botany.
Greene's (G. W.) Companion to Ollendorff.
—— First Lessons in French.
—— First Lessons in Italian.
—— Middle Ages.
Gregory's Mathematics.
Griffin on the Gospel.
Griffith's Poems.
Griswold's Republican Court.
——— Sacred Poets.
Guizot's (Madame) Tales.
Guizot's (M.) Civilization in Europe. 4 vols.
—— School edition. 1 vol.
—— New Edition, on tinted paper. 4 vols.
Gurowski's America and Europe.
——— Russia as it is.

Hadley's Greek Grammar.
Hahn's Greek Testament.
Hall's (B. H.) Eastern Vermont.
Hall's (C. H.) Notes on the Gospels. 2 vols.
Hall's (E. H.) Guide to the Great West.
Halleck's Poems.
—— Poems. Pocket size, blue and gold.
—— Young America.
Halleck's (H. W.) Military Science.
Hamilton's (Sir Wm.) Philosophy.
Hamilton's (A.) Writings. 6 vols.

Hand-Books on Education.
Hand-Book of Anglo-Saxon Root-Words.
Hand-Book of Anglo-Saxon Derivatives.
Hand-Book of the Engrafted Words.
Handy-Book of Property Law.
Happy Child's Library. 18 vols. in case.
Harkness' First Greek Book.
—— Latin Grammar.
—— First Latin Book.
—— Second "
—— Latin Reader.
Hase's History of the Church.
Haskell's Housekeeper's Encyclopædia.
Hassard's Life of Archbishop Hughes.
—— Wreath of Beauty.
Haupt on Bridge Construction.
Haven's Where There's a Will There's a Way.
—— Patient Waiting no Loss.
—— Nothing Venture Nothing Have.
—— Out of Debt Out of Danger.
—— Contentment Better than Wealth.
—— No Such Word as Fail.
—— All's Not Gold that Glitters.
—— A Place for Everything, and Everything in its Place.
—— Loss and Gain.
—— Pet Bird.
—— Home Series of Juvenile Books. 8 vols. in case.
Haven (Memoir of Alice B.).
Hazard on the Will.
Hecker's Questions of the Soul.
Hemans' Poems. 2 vols.
—— Songs of the Affections.
Henck's Field-Book for Engineers.
Henry on Human Progress.
Herbert's Poems.
Here and There.
Herodotus, by Johnson (in Greek).
Herodotus, by Rawlinson (in English). 4 vols.
Heydenreich's German Reader.
Hickok's Rational Cosmology.
—— Rational Psychology.
History of the Rebellion, Military and Naval. Illustrated.
Hoffman's Poems.
Holcombe's Leading Cases.
—— Law of Dr. and Cr.
—— Letters in Literature.
Holly's Country Seats.
Holmes' (M. A.) Tempest and Sunshine.
—— English Orphans.
Holmes' (A.) Parties and Principles.
Homes of American Authors.
Homer's Iliad.
Hooker's Complete Works. 2 vols.
Hoppin's Notes.
Horace, edited by Lincoln.
Howitt's Child's Verse-Book.
—— Juvenile Tales. 14 vols. in case.
How's Historical Shakspearian Reader.
—— Shakspearian Reader.
Huc's Tartary and China.
Hudson's Life and Adventures.
Humboldt's Letters.
Hunt's (C. H.) Life of Livingston.
Hunt's (F. W.) Historical Atlas.
Huntington's Lady Alice.
Hutton's Mathematics.
Huxley's Man's Place in Nature.
—— Origin of Species.

Iconographic Encyclopædia. 6 vols.—4 Text and 2 Plates.
Or, separately:
The Countries and Cities of the World. 2 vols.
The Navigation of all Ages. 2 vols.
The Art of Building in Ancient and Modern Times. 2 vols.
The Religions of Ancient and Modern Times. 2 vols.
The Fine Arts Illustrated. 2 vols.
Technology Illustrated. 2 vols.
Internal Revenue Law.
Iredell's Life. 2 vols.
Italian Comedies.

Jacobs' Learning to Spell.
—— The same, in two parts.
Jaeger's Class-Book of Zoology.
James' (J. A.) Young Man.
James' (H.) Logic of Creation.
James' (G. P. R.) Adrien.
Jameson's (Mrs.) Art Works.
—— Legends of Saints and Martyrs. 2 vols.
—— Legends of the Monastic Orders.
—— Legends of the Madonna.
—— History of Our Lord. 2 vols.
Jarvis' Reply to Milner.
Jay on American Agriculture.
Jeffers on Gunnery.
Jeffrey's (F.) Essays.
Johnson's Meaning of Words.
Johnson's (Samuel) Rasselas.
Johnston's Chemistry of Common Life. 2 vols.

Kavanagh's Adele.
—— Beatrice.
—— Daisy Burns.
—— Grace Lee.
—— Madeleine.
—— Nathalie.
—— Rachel Gray.
—— Seven Years.
—— Queen Mab.
—— Women of Christianity.
Keats' Poems.

Keep a Good Heart.
Keightley's Mythology.
Keil's Fairy Stories.
Keith (Memoir of Caroline P.)
Kendrick's Greek Ollendorff.
Kenny's Manual of Chess.
Kinglake's Crimean War. Vols. 1 and 2.
Kirke White's Poems.
Kirkland's Life of Washington.
A Cheaper Edition, for Schools.
Knowles' Orlean Lamar.
Kœppen's Middle Ages.
—— Separately—Middle Ages, 2 vols.
——— Atlas.
Kohlrausch's History of Germany.
Kuhner's Greek Grammar.

Lafever's Beauties of Architecture.
Lady Alice.
Lamartine's Confidential Disclosures.
——— History of Turkey. 3 vols.
Lancelott's Queens of England, and their Times. 2 vols.
Landon's (L. E.) Complete Works.
Latham's English Language.
Layard's Nineveh. Illustrated.
—— Cheap edition. Without Illustrations.
Learning to Spell.
Le Brun's Telemaque.
Lecky's Rise and Influence of Rationalism. 2 vols.
Le Sage's Adventures of Gil Blas. 1 vol.
—— Gil Blas, in Spanish.
Letter Writer.
Letters from Rome.
Lewes' (G. H.) History of Philosophy. 2 vols.
—— In 1 vol.
—— Physiology of Common Life.
Library of Travel and Adventure. 3 vols. in case.
Library for my Young Countrymen. 9 vols. in case.
Libro Primario de Ortografia.
Liebig's Laws of Husbandry.
Life of Man Symbolized by the Months of the Year.
Light and Darkness
Lights and Shadows of New York Picture Galleries.
Lindsay's Poems.
Linn's Life and Services.
Little Builder.
Little Engineer.
Livy, with English Notes.
Logan's Château Frissac.
Looking Glass for the Mind.
Lord's Poems.
—— Christ in Hades: a Poem.
Louise.
Lunt's Origin of the Late War.
Lyell's Elements of Geology.
Lyell's Principles of Geology.
Lyra Americana.
Lyra Anglicana.

Macaulay's Essays. 1 vol.
—— Essays. 7 vols.
—— Essays. A New and Revised Edition, on tinted paper. 6 vols.
Mackintosh's (Sir James) Essays.
Madge.
Mahan's Answer to Colenso.
—— Numerals of Scripture.
Mahon's England. 2 vols.
Maiu's Novum Testamentum Græce.
Mandeville's New Series of Readers.
1. Primary Reader.
2. Second Reader.
3. Third Reader
4. Fourth Reader.
5. Fifth Reader.
Mandeville's Course of Reading.
——— Reading and Oratory.
——— First Spanish Reader.
——— Second Spanish Reader.
——— Third Spanish Reader.
Magnall's Historical Questions.
Man's Cry and God's Gracious Answer.
Manners' At Home and Abroad.
——— Sedgemoor.
Manning's Temporal Mission of the Holy Ghost.
——— The Reunion of Christendom.
Manual of Matrimony.
Markham's History of England.
Marrayat's Africa.
——— Masterman Ready.
——— Popular Novels. 12 vols.
——— A New and Revised Edition, printed on tinted paper 12 vols.
Marryat's Settlers in Canada.
Marshall's (E. C.) Book of Oratory.
——— First Book of Oratory.
Marshall's (T. W.) Notes on Episcopacy.
Marsh's Double Entry Book-keeping.
—— Single Entry Book-keeping.
—— Bank Book-keeping.
—— Book-keeping (in Spanish).
—— Blank Books for Double Entry. 6 books in set.
—— Do. for Single Entry. 6 books in set.
Martha's Hooks and Eyes.
Martineau's Crofton Boys.
——— Peasant and Prince.
Mary Lee.
Mary Staunton.
Mathews on Whist.
Mayhew's Illustrated Horse Doctor.
May's Bertram Noel.
—— Louis' School Days.
—— Mortimer's College Life.
—— Sunshine of Greystone.
McCormick's Visit to Sebastopol.

McIntosh's Aunt Kitty's Tales.
—— Charms and Counter Charms.
—— Evenings at Donaldson Manor.
—— Lofty and Lowly. 2 vols.
—— Maggie and Emma.
—— Meta Gray.
—— Two Lives.
—— Two Pictures.
—— New Juvenile Library. 7 vols. in case.
McLee's Alphabets.
McWhorter's Church Essays.
Meadows' Italian Dictionary.
Memoirs of Catharine II.
Merchant of Venice.
Merivale's History of the Romans. 7 vols.
Conversion of the Roman Empire.
" " Northern Nations.
Merry Christmas Book.
Michelet's France. 2 vols.
Milhouse's Italian Dictionary. 2 vols.
Mill's Political Economy. 2 vols.
Milledulcia.
Milton's Poems.
—— Paradise Lost.
Miniature Library. 27 vols.
Ministry of Life.
Minturn's Travels in India.
Modern British Essayists. 8 vols.
Modet's Light.
Moore's Revolutionary Ballads.
Moore's (George H.) Notes on the History of Slavery in Massachusetts.
Moore's (Thos.) Irish Melodies.
Moore's (Thos.) Memoirs and Journal. 2 vols.
—— Lallah Rookh.
—— Poems. 1 vol., cheap edition.
—— Do., on fine tinted paper.
Morales' Spanish Reader.
Moran on Money.
More's Practical Piety. 2 vols.
—— Private Devotions.
—— Domestic Tales.
—— Rural Tales.
—— Village Tales. 2 vols. in 1.
Morin's Practical Mechanics.
Morphy's Chess Games.
—— Triumphs.
Mulligan's English Grammar.
My Cave Life in Vicksburg.

Napoleon Bonaparte, by F. de l'Ardeche.
Napoleon Correspondence. 2 vols.
New Fairy Stories.
Newcomb on Financial Policy.
Newman's Apologia Pro Vita Sua.
—— Sermons.
New Testament, with engravings on wood from designs by the ancient masters. 1 vol.
New Testament, with Comment by E. Churton and W. B. Jones. 2 vols.
New York City Banks.
New York Picture Galleries.
Nightcap Series of Juveniles. 6 vols. in case.
Nightingale on Nursing.
Novum Testamentum, interprete Beza.
Nueva Biblioteca de la Risa.
Nuovo Tesoro di Schergos.
Nursery Basket.

O'Callaghan's New Netherlands. 2 vols.
Œhlschlager's German Reader.
Ogilby on Lay Baptism.
Oldfellow's Uncle Nat.
Oliphant's Katmandu.
Ollendorff's English Grammar foi Spaniards.
A Key to the Exercises.
—— English Grammar for Germans.
A Key to the Exercises.
—— French Grammar, by Jewett.
A Key to the Exercises.
—— French Grammar, by Value.
A Key to the Exercises.
—— French Grammar for Spaniards.
Key to the same.
—— German Grammar.
A Key to the Exercises.
—— Italian Grammar.
A Key to the Exercises.
—— Spanish Grammar.
A Key to the Exercises.
Ortografia.
Ordronaux' Hints on Health.
Oriental Library. 5 vols. in case.
Osgood's Hearthstone.
—— Mile Stones.
Ostervald's Nouveau Testament.
Otis' Landscapes. 1 vol.
—— The same, in 6 parts.
—— Studies of Animals. 1 vol.
—— Studies of Animals. 6 parts.
Overman's Metallurgy.
Owen's (Jno. J.) Acts of the Apostles.
—— Greek Reader.
—— Homer's Odyssey.
—— Homer's Iliad.
—— Thucydides.
—— Xenophon's Anabasis.
—— Xenophon's Cyropædia.
Owen's Penmanship. 3 books.

Paez' Geografia del Mundo.
Pages and Pictures. From the writings of James Fenimore Cooper.
Paine's Tent and Harem.
Palenzuela's Gramatica Inglesa.
Key to the same.
Palmer's Book-keeping.

Parker's Critical and Miscellaneous Writings.
—— Speeches and Addresses. 3 vols.
—— Additional Speeches. 2 vols.
—— Sermons of Theism.
—— Ten Sermons.
—— Trial and Defence.
—— Two Christmas Celebrations.
—— Works. 2 vols.
—— (Life of Theodore). 2 vols.
Parley's Faggots for the Fireside.
—— Present for all Seasons.
Parley's Wanderers by Sea and Land.
Patton's History of the United States.
Paul and Virginia.
Pearson on the Creed.
Perkins' Primary Arithmetic.
—— Elementary Arithmetic.
—— Practical Arithmetic.
—— The same, in Spanish.
—— A Key to Practical Arithmetic.
—— Higher Arithmetic.
—— Algebra.
—— Higher Algebra.
—— Geometry.
—— Higher Geometry.
—— Plane Trigonometry.
Perry's Americans in Japan.
—— Expedition to the China Seas and Japan.
Petit's Household Mysteries.
Peyrac's Comment on Parle à Paris.
Phelan on Billiards.
Phœnixiana.
Picture Gallery, in Spanish.
Pickell's Narrative. History of the Potomac Company.
Planches' Lead Diseases.
Plato's Apology.
Poetical Gems. Blue and Gold. 6 vols. in case.
Poets' Gallery.
Pollok's Poems.
Pomeroy's Municipal Law.
Pope's Poems.
Porter's Scottish Chiefs.
Portraits of my Married Friends.
Practical Cook Book.
Pratt's Dawnings of Genius.
Prince Charlie.
Pulpit Cyclopædia and Minister's Companion.
Punch's Pocket-Book of Fun.
Punchinello.
Pure Gold.
Pusey's Eirenicon.
Putz's Ancient Geography.
—— Mediæval Geography.
—— Modern Geography.

Quackenbos' First Book in English Grammar.
—— English Grammar.
—— First Lessons on Composition.
Quackenbos' Advanced Course of Composition and Rhetoric.
—— Natural Philosophy.
—— Primary History.
—— History of the United States.
—— Primary Arithmetic.
—— Elementary Arithmetic.
—— Practical Arithmetic.
Queens of England: a Series of Portraits.

Railway Anecdote Book.
Rawlinson's Herodotus. 4 vols.
Recreative Readings in French.
Reid's English Dictionary.
Reminiscences of a Zouave.
Replies to Essays and Reviews.
Republican Court.
Report on the Hygienic Condition of New York City.
Report of the United States Revenue Commission.
Reynard the Fox. After the version of Goethe.
Reynolds on Hand-Railings.
Rice's (Harvey) Poems.
Richards' At Home and Abroad.
—— Pleasure and Profit.
—— Harry's Vacation.
—— Electron.
Ricord's Youth's Grammar.
Ripalda's Spanish Catechism.
Robbins' Book of Poetry.
—— Guide to Knowledge.
Robertson's English Course for Spaniards, with Key.
Roemer's First French Reader.
—— Second French Reader.
—— Polyglot Readers—comprising English Text; French, German, Spanish, and Italian Translations.
Rosa Mystica.
Rosales' Caton Christiana.
Round the Block.
Rowan's French Reader.
—— French Revolution. 2 vols.
Royo's Instruccion Moral.

St. Pierre's Paul and Virginia.
Saintaine's Picciola. (In French.)
Sallust, with Notes.
Sampson's Brief Remarker.
Sandham's Twin Sisters.
Sanitary Condition of New York.
Sarmiento's Lectura Gradual.
Savarin's Hand-Book of Dining.
Schedel's Emancipation of Faith. 2 vols.
Schmidt's Ancient Geography.
Schmucker's History of the Four Georges.
Schwegler's History of Philosophy.
Scott's Lady of the Lake.
—— Lay of the Last Minstrel.

www.ingramcontent.com/pod-product-compliance
Lightning Source LLC
LaVergne TN
LVHW020312110826
845148LV00017BA/389